MAYBERRY FIRSTS

A Compendium of
Historical Essays on the
Classic Television Series

RANDY TURNER

LIBERTY GROVE PRESS LLC
GREATER CINCINNATI

Liberty Grove Press LLC
P.O. Box 145
West Chester, OH 45071

Cover photo of the original candlestick phone prop by Tim Bradshaw.

Photos of the Mayberry Trading Post, Fife Avenue sign, and Snappy Lunch sign by Randy Turner. All other interior photographs are used for illustrative purposes pursuant to the Fair Use Doctrine and are reproduced for commentary, critical, and scholarly purposes.

Cover design by Bethart Printing Solutions.

This book is not connected with *The Andy Griffith Show* nor has it been created, licensed, authorized, or endorsed by any of the series creators and owners or their successors in interest.

First Printing, September 2019

4 5 6 7 8 9 10 11 12

ISBN # 978-0-578-53339-1

Printed in the United States of America.

Dedicated to Cecilia
for her steadfast love and support
and to Elise and Allison
for being the best dang daughters
in the whole dang world.

Contents

Preface

When *The Andy Griffith Show* premiered, I was too young to remember it. I do remember seeing new episodes during the color years and seeing reruns of the black and white episodes. I rediscovered the show in college and have been a fan ever since.

I still marvel at the quality of the series produced in an era where a season consisted of 32 episodes per year. The show likely would never be given a green light for production by a studio today. The pacing is unlike anything else on the air. I am as big a fan of current shows as anyone, but when it comes to comedies, it seems to me that most are now based on tearing someone else down. The "humor" most often comes at another character's expense.

Mayberry was instead about people watching out for one another. The quiet, reflective moments such as Malcolm Tucker falling asleep on the front porch or serious scenes such as Andy talking with Opie about Mr. McBeevee simply do not exist in current television situation comedies.

That is undoubtedly one of the reasons the show endures.

2020 marked the sixtieth anniversary of *The Andy Griffith Show*'s debut. The series never left the top 10 in Nielsen rankings during its eight-year run and was the number one show in the country during its final season. Thanks to syndicated airings, *The Andy Griffith Show* has never been off the air. It draws millions of viewers when broadcast on channels in spite of those episodes being butchered with vital scenes removed to make room for the greater number of commercials shown in each time slot than was the case in the 1960s. The show is available in digital formats through both discs and streaming. Festivals attended by tens of thousands are held every year that are not sponsored by the original studio but instead are fan-driven. *The Andy Griffith Show* will never be repeated.

Several people are especially deserving of a sincere note of thanks and gratitude for their generous assistance.

Thanks to Tim Bradshaw for use of his photograph on the cover. Tim took this photo of the actual candlestick telephone prop used during the filming of *The Andy Griffith Show* at the beautiful Andy Griffith Museum in Griffith's hometown of Mount Airy, North Carolina where it is just one of the many treasures on permanent display. Becoming friends with Tim has been one of the wonderful benefits of my involvement in the Mayberry community.

I am grateful to director Bruce Bilson who served as Assistant Director during the first two seasons of *The Andy Griffith Show*. Mr. Bilson was kind and gracious in discussing several aspects of his time on the show about which I had questions.

Peggy Barkley, the proprietor of the Mayberry Trading Post, has never failed to offer me great kindness and extreme generosity in her sharing of valuable information.

Thanks to Nancy Chifala of Nancy Chifala Design for her expert advice on the cover design and to John Houchin and Rob Carper of Bethart Printing Solutions for their generous advice and help with the cover and the overall book design.

My dear friend Ann Porter provided a valuable suggestion of the right approach to be taken in the writing of the essays.

The knowledgable staff at Louis Round Wilson Special Collections Library at the University of North Carolina-Chapel Hill are thanked for their generous assistance.

Special thanks to my wife, Cecilia, and daughter, Elise, for their invaluable help in refining the wording for the information included on the covers of *Mayberry Firsts*.

And finally, a most heartfelt expression of thanks is extended to Matt Hurley for his generous review of this book. A true expert on trivia related to *The Andy Griffith Show*, Matt offered input where needed and encouragement on all of the short-form essays that make up *Mayberry Firsts*.

Long live Mayberry!

Randy Turner
June 2019

When did The Andy Griffith Show first come into being?

Andy Griffith was already well known before he appeared in Mayberry. Among his many accomplishments were the popular recording of his comedy monologue "What It Was, Was Football," his starring role in Elia Kazan's masterful film *A Face in the Crowd*, and his Tony-nominated performance as Will Stockdale in *No Time for Sergeants*. The Broadway show was adapted as a hit film, also starring Griffith, but his follow-up film *Onionhead* was a flop. While he again earned a Tony nomination for his portrayal of the title role in *Destry Rides Again*, ticket sales were not strong. Between *Onionhead* and *Destry*, Griffith was convinced he needed to try television.

Griffith and his manager, Richard O. Linke, approached the legendary agent and president of the William Morris Agency Abe Lastfogel who represented actors such as Frank Sinatra and Marilyn Monroe and who was responsible for the agency expanding to Hollywood and overseas. Lastfogel was also the agent for Danny Thomas with the two being so close that Thomas often referred to Lastfogel as "Uncle Abe." Linke and Griffith explained Griffith's desire to work in television. This led Lastfogel to contact the acclaimed television producer Sheldon Leonard and ask if he would be interested in developing a series for Griffith. Among his already impressive accomplishments, Leonard was an Executive Producer of *The Danny Thomas Show* which had originally been titled *Make Room for Daddy*.

Leonard was indeed interested as he was already familiar with Griffith and began working on a series concept. After kicking around various ideas with a writer and editor for *The Danny*

Thomas Show, Arthur "Artie" Stander, Leonard decided the best pitch would be to have Griffith play a character in a rural setting since he was known for a rural style of comedy.

In the winter of 1959, Leonard traveled to New York City to watch Griffith perform in *Destry Rides Again*, then went backstage to introduce himself. He took Griffith to one of Griffith's favorite nearby bars and, over a beer and a sandwich, told him his idea of a series in which Griffith would play the sheriff of a small Southern town. While the exact date is unknown, Sheldon Leonard had created what was to be known as *The Andy Griffith Show*.

However, a deal was not immediate. Griffith insisted on multiple meetings between himself, Linke, and Leonard, surprising Leonard that he wasn't jumping at the chance to potentially star in his own series. But after the third meeting, Griffith and Leonard shook hands to agree that *The Andy Griffith Show* would become a reality.

Of course, the fully realized show is the product of many people. Leonard's acknowledgment of Stander's contributions vary. Regardless, it was Stander who wrote the script for the pilot episode which aired on February 15, 1960, as an episode of *The Danny Thomas Show*. The show had already been picked up by sponsor General Foods before it ever aired. *The Andy Griffith Show* debuted on CBS on October 3, 1960.

When was Andy Taylor first seen?

The answer seems obvious but it actually depends on whether one considers the pilot episode to be canon, a genuine episode that is part of the same "Mayberry Universe" as *The Andy Griffith Show*; its two successful spin-offs, *Gomer Pyle-USMC* and *Mayberry R.F.D.*; and the later made-for-television reunion movie, *Return to Mayberry*.

If one takes the pilot as canon, then Andy Taylor was first seen on February 15, 1960, in the episode of *The Danny Thomas Show* titled "Danny Meets Andy Griffith." There are significant differences in the Mayberry seen in the pilot and the next time Andy Taylor was seen on October 3, 1960, in "The New Housekeeper," the first episode of *The Andy Griffith Show*. Physically, the little bit the audience sees of Main Street in the pilot is different from what is seen in the series and the courthouse itself, while similar, is also not the same.

There is no Aunt Bee. Instead, Andy and Opie are cared for by Andy's unseen Aunt Lucy. There is a "town drunk" who lets himself in the jail cell but it is not Otis, it is Will Hoople. Just as in *The Andy Griffith Show*, Andy is both the Mayberry Sheriff and Justice of the Peace, but in the pilot, he is also the editor of the local paper.

Still, in many ways, Andy is the same in *The Andy Griffith Show* as he was in the pilot. He is still the widowed father of his young son, Opie. He is clearly a character that may be from a rural, small town but whose common sense and innate goodness triumph when confronted with arrogant attitudes just as they did when dealing with the cocky "city slicker" Danny Williams in the pilot. In addition, when considering canon, one must acknowledge that the regular series is full of inconsistencies with missing courthouse windows, backdrops on set the first season that do not represent what the town looks like in exterior shots, changing dates of high school graduations at class reunions, different middle names given for Barney, and the like. Yet all the episodes that are part of the original series are clearly canon, inconsistencies notwithstanding.

So truly, the answer depends on the viewer's individual outlook. The character of Sheriff Andy Taylor by name appeared in February in the pilot, but some might argue that the "real" character did not appear until October in the series.

There is no way to authoritatively verify the origin of the name "Taylor" but Andy Griffith was known to often use the names of relatives and people he knew as character names in *The Andy Griffith Show*. It is quite likely Griffith chose "Taylor" because it is the maiden name of his paternal grandmother and, by extension, the surname of his paternal great grandfather.

When was the town of Mayberry first referenced?

The name "Mayberry" is first seen in the opening shot of the pilot episode as Andy Taylor and Danny Williams with his family pull up in their cars. A sign on a post outside a building reads "Mayberry Courthouse and Jail." The name "Mayberry" is first spoken when Danny says he would like to call the local newspaper to expose Andy for giving him a larger than average fine. After Danny says, "I'd call the paper right here if you had one in this little hickville," Andy responds they have "a outstanding paper—the *Mayberry Gazette.*"

In the ongoing series before any of the starring actors are seen, the establishing shot shows the "Mayberry Courthouse" sign above the entryway with "Sheriff" and "Justice of the Peace" signs on the doors. The first person to speak the name "Mayberry" in the series is Andy when he refers to the power given to him as Justice of the Peace of Mayberry when performing the marriage of Rose and Wilbur. Barney also uses the town's name in the first episode when expressing his concern that Mayberry could turn into a regular "sin town."

Andy Griffith denied for decades that his hometown of Mount Airy, North Carolina was an influence on the fictional town of Mayberry. The producers instilled a sense of nostalgia in the television series by giving Mayberry a feel of the 1930s, the years of Griffith's childhood, even though the series is set in the 1960s. Griffith also frequently made references in the show to real family names from Mount Airy, specific locations in the town, and actual businesses such as Mount Airy's Snappy Lunch diner. So it is not surprising that many feel the fictional Mayberry was based on Griffith's childhood hometown.

While never specifically stating that the fictional Mayberry was modeled after Mount Airy, Griffith did finally admit on October 16, 2002, while attending the Andy Griffith Highway dedication ceremony, it was at least a partial influence. The fictional Mayberry was obviously not based directly on any town as such idyllic perfection never existed. Fans may love Mayberry partially because it reminds them of a simpler time, but Griffith and the show's producers never intended it to be an accurate depiction of life in a small, Southern town. Still, since Mount Airy is the town where Griffith was raised, it would actually be surprising for it not to have been at least some influence.

Similarly, Griffith always denied he had anything to do with coming up with the name "Mayberry" for the show, saying it was an invention of either show creator Sheldon Leonard or writer Artie Stander who wrote the pilot episode.

However, time has revealed this is highly unlikely. An actual community called Mayberry is near Mount Airy not far over the state line in Virginia. That alone would suggest it is the origin of the name, as it would be an incredible coincidence that Leonard who was born in Manhattan or Stander who was born in the Bronx would have coincidentally fabricated a name for the town that was also the name of a real community so near Griffith's hometown. Later events seem incontrovertible.

Sam and Jopina Frances Nunn, Andy Griffith's maternal grandparents, lived in the Mayberry community atop a nearby mountain. Thus, Griffith's mother lived in the community of Mayberry as a child. Records at the Mayberry Trading Post, a general store in the community that has been operating since 1892, reveal that Griffith's maternal grandparents traded at the store and that Griffith's grandfather used to sell the store owner chestnuts he had gathered. Betty Lynn, the actress who played Thelma Lou, actually visited the store shortly after she moved to Mount Airy upon retirement. She revealed to the owner that Griffith spoke to her about the community of Mayberry many times during the filming of the series. He had told her about the "real Mayberry" so she said she came to the store as she wanted to see the community Griffith had told her about so many years before.

Describing the building, Peggy Barkley, the former proprietor of the Mayberry Trading Post, points out if you were over 125 years old, you would lean, too.

When was Opie Taylor first seen?

The underlying concept of *The Andy Griffith Show* was always that of a widowed father raising his young son. This is especially obvious with the lack of a deputy in the pilot. Certainly, Barney Fife became an important element of the show's success during the first five black and white seasons, but the producers never lost sight of the primary importance of the father-son relationship.

Knowing that they needed to find an exceptional child actor for the upcoming pilot episode, producer Sheldon Leonard was searching. On the evening of December 20, 1959, he saw a performance by five-year-old Ronny Howard in an episode of the anthology show *General Electric Theater* and immediately knew he had found Opie.

The episode Leonard had seen was titled "Mr. O'Malley." It was based on the popular 1940s comic strip *Barnaby*. Howard played Barnaby while the title character, a cigar-smoking fairy godfather, was played by Bert Lahr who had played the Cowardly Lion in *The Wizard of Oz*. The following day, Leonard contacted Howard's agent and learned "Mr. O'Malley" was intended as a pilot for a possible series. He told the agent if the pilot was not picked up—which Leonard did not think would be—he wanted Howard for the role of Opie. The proposed *Mr. O'Malley* series did not go forward.

Howard's parents were hesitant to allow their son to be one of the lead characters in an ongoing series with a long term contract. Ron Howard's father, Rance Howard, told Leonard he and his wife felt Ronny deserved to have a childhood. Leonard promised Ronny would have as normal a life as possible and that the show's producers would go out of their way to provide Ronny everything needed to have an authentic childhood.

An additional point of assurance for Howard's parents was that, while the relationship between a father and his son would often be a focal point of the show, Ronny would not be the main lead in the way that Jay North was in *Dennis the Menace* or Jerry Mathers was in *Leave It to Beaver*. Some episodes would feature Ronny heavily, but there would be only five or so episodes of that type per year, not all 32. In fact, occasionally Ronny would even have episodes off in which he did not appear at all. His parents decided to allow him to take the role.

Opie was first seen on February 15, 1960, in the pilot episode "Danny Meets Andy Griffith" in *The Danny Thomas Show*. Opie comes into the courthouse upset that his pet turtle Wilford is dead, having been accidentally stepped on by Mrs. Bolivar. He tearfully says he wants Andy to arrest her, give her a fair trial, and then hang her.

Ronny Howard did not have an audition but does remember later being taken to meet producer Aaron Ruben before the series began. He has said his most vivid memory of the interview was Ruben's amusement that he was still so small that he could stand under Ruben's desk without hitting his head.

When *The Andy Griffith Show* premiered on October 3, 1960, the establishing shot is of the courthouse door. As the camera zooms into the Justice of the Peace sign, the image dissolves to show Andy as the first character seen. As that same shot then pulls back, the next character's face seen is Opie's. This was not an accident. Series-creator Leonard knew what the series was about and it was Leonard who directed the first episode.

Leonard had already directed Griffith and Howard in another

scenario that was not part of the story told in the first episode. He directed the opening and closing credits. The credits show Andy and Opie walking along a country path beside a lake on a fishing trip. They are the only two characters seen in the credits during the entire eight-year run of the series.

Ronny Howard always had second billing in the series. While Don Knotts as Barney Fife became an important part of the series, the actor never received higher than third billing.

The unusual name of "Opie" came from Opie Cates, a popular clarinetist and bandleader who also worked as a radio actor. "Opie" was a nickname for Opal, Cates' actual first name. Leonard was a cast member in the 1940s radio comedy *Meet Me at Parky's* which also included "Opie Cates and his Orchestra." Both Leonard and Griffith were fans of the classic radio series *Lum and Abner* in which Cates also sometimes appeared. Both being fans of Cates, they decided to use the name for Andy Taylor's son.

When was Andy's first love interest seen?

The first of several attempts to give Andy a girlfriend was the introduction of Elinor Donahue as Ellie Walker early in the first season. Ellie is first seen in the fourth episode, "Ellie Comes to Town," as the newly-graduated "pharmacy gal" niece of Fred Walker who runs Walker's Drugstore.

Donahue's break into stardom came when she was cast as Betty "Princess" Anderson, the oldest daughter, in *Father Knows Best* (1954-1960), the role for which she is best known to non-Mayberry fans. She came to Mayberry fresh from the conclusion of that series. Donahue was under a three-year contract with *The Andy Griffith Show*. The producer's original plan was for Andy to court Ellie during the first season, for the couple to become engaged during the second season, and to marry during the third. The plan was changed when the hoped-for chemistry between the characters did not materialize and Griffith let it be known there would be no on-screen marriage. Donahue agreed, saying the show would have then become something closer to *Sheriff Knows Best*.

Donahue was hired as a series regular and received billing above Don Knotts in episodes in which she appeared, with the announcer saying, "Also starring Elinor Donahue and Don Knotts." However, as it became clear the chemistry between Griffith and Donahue was lacking, she ultimately appeared in less than half the first season episodes. She played Ellie in only 12 of the season's 32 episodes. Even allowing for the fact that the character was not introduced until the fourth episode, she still appeared in just over 40% of the episodes after she was introduced.

A large part of the problem was the 11-year age difference between the actors. The public remembered Donahue as a college student in *Father Knows Best* just a few months earlier. This likely contributed to the awkwardness of signs of affection between the two, coupled with Griffith's admission he had trouble playing love scenes, a fact which is evident throughout the entire series. Additionally, Donahue never claimed to be a comedian and the famous chemistry between Griffith and Knotts resulted in lines given to her character in a script being shifted to Knotts during table reads, decisions she has said she understood and with which she agreed.

Realizing herself that the situation was not working as planned, Donahue asked to be released from her three-year contract at the conclusion of the first season. As was typical for the series, when she did leave her absence was simply never referenced with viewers left to assume their relationship had ended and she had moved away. Regardless, Ellie is the favorite of Andy Taylor's girlfriends among many fans.

The character shared the first name with the actress who

portrayed her, including the unusual spelling of her first name which was seen as she hung her diploma. The surname Walker is said to have been an homage to one of Andy Griffith's friends John Walker.

When did Andy first underestimate Opie?

While Andy Taylor is viewed by many fans as close to the ideal father figure, his occasional underestimation of Opie was a theme that recurred several times.

This was first seen on November 28, 1960, in the eighth episode of the new series. In "Opie's Charity," Andy is embarrassed to learn that Opie has donated only three cents to the Underprivileged Children's Charity Drive conducted by Annabelle Silby. Opie has $2.20 in his piggy bank so Andy tries a variety of methods to convince Opie he should be more generous, including explaining to him that he read there were 400 needy boys in the county alone, which was one and a half boys per square mile. Opie is confused, never having seen a half a boy. Andy explains, "Well, it's not really a half a boy. It's a ratio." Opie asks, "Horatio who?" Realizing that trying to explain the mathematics to his young son is futile, Andy tells him to just forget about the half a boy. Opie says, "It's pretty hard to forget a thing like that, Pa." He then thoughtfully adds, "Poor Horatio."

Opie later explains he can't give any more money since he needs to spend it on his girlfriend, Charlotte. Andy tells Opie how important it is to share with those not as lucky as he is. When Opie continues to say he can't give more, Andy sends him to his room without supper, saying to himself he would be a laughing stock in town with such a stingy son. After Aunt Bee points out the hypocrisy of Andy condemning Annabelle Silby for being so concerned with what others thought that she had told people her husband had died when he had, in fact, left her, Andy calls Opie back down for supper. When Andy learns Opie is saving his money to buy his girlfriend a new coat because hers is worn out and her mother can't afford to buy her a new one, Andy realizes he has underestimated his son. He says that while Opie and Aunt Bee are having fried chicken for supper, he is having crow.

"Opie's Charity" is an example of a storytelling method now commonplace but at the time unusual. The episode consists of two distinct and intertwined storylines: Andy trying to convince Opie to donate more money and Andy learning that Annabelle's husband, Tom, is not really dead.

Two seasons later in the third season opener, Andy once again doubts Opie in the classic episode "Mr. McBeevee." After pretending to have an imaginary horse, Opie meets a telephone lineman named McBeevee. When he later describes McBeevee to Andy and Barney using childlike terms, such as saying his friend walks in the treetops, and repeats McBeevee's own fanciful terms, such as referring to his tool belt as his twelve extra hands, Andy insists Opie admit McBeevee is make-believe. In one of the most moving scenes of the series, Andy at first tells Opie he will get a spanking if he doesn't admit he made up McBeevee. In a wonderfully acted moment as played by the talented young Ronny Howard, Opie can't bring himself to lie and tearfully asks his pa if he doesn't believe him. Andy does not spank him and afterward tells Barney and Aunt Bee he doesn't believe in Mr. McBeevee but he does believe in Opie. When Andy then goes to the woods himself and ends up meeting the telephone lineman, he is elated to learn McBeevee is real and quickly realizes he had misunderstood Opie's descriptions.

In Season 5, Andy again underestimates Opie in "Opie's Fortune." After Opie finds a man's change purse with $50 in it and it goes unclaimed for a week, Opie is told the money is his and is allowed to spend $10 with $40 put in a new piggy bank. Barney then sees a lost-and-found ad placed by Parnell Rigsby who had lost the change purse. Rather than disappoint Opie, Andy covers the $50 himself and leaves to return the purse and money to Rigsby. Meanwhile, Opie buys a new fishing rod and brings it to the courthouse but finds no one there. Rigsby then comes in and tells Opie he is checking to see if someone had turned in his lost purse. Even though he had been told by Andy the money is legally his, Opie still breaks his piggy bank so he can return the $40. Meanwhile, Andy and Barney have returned the purse and met Rigsby who told them he had just left a message about it with Opie at the courthouse. Again underestimating Opie, when Andy finds the broken piggy bank he believes Opie is on a spending spree. He finds Opie in the sporting goods store where he had bought the fishing rod. When he learns Opie was not spending more money in the store and was instead returning the fishing rod to get the other $10 back, Andy realizes his mistake, rhetorically asking, "Well, I did it again, didn't I?"

The concept was used one last time in the sixth season opener and first color episode, "Opie's Job." Opie and a new boy in town vie to be hired for a part-time job at the market now run by Mr. Doakes. (The grocer was played by Norris Goff who had played Abner Peabody on one of Andy Griffith's favorite radio comedies, *Lum and Abner*.) After Opie wins the competition, he learns the other boy was trying to get the job because his father has been sick and his family has bills to pay. Opie then intentionally gets fired so the other boy can have the job and needed income. Once an angry Andy learns the truth, he apologizes to Opie. He tells him, "You know, when I was braggin' on you to Floyd and Goober, I told them how proud I was to have a boy like you. But that's not quite true. You're a man."

When was Andy's deceased wife first referenced?

Since *The Andy Griffith Show* was first and foremost a comedy, albeit with the occasional serious scene, Andy's deceased wife is understandably only referenced a few times.

In the pilot episode aired February 15, 1960, New York entertainer Danny Williams is serving a ten-day sentence rather than pay what he believes at the time is an unfair fine. Up to that point, Danny has thought little of Andy whom he calls a hick, mocking his Southern accent. Danny first gains some insight into Andy as a real person when Opie comes into the courthouse, upset as his pet turtle, Wilford, is dead. Opie says Wilford has been murdered. He says that while in the ice cream parlor, Mrs. Bolivar stepped on Wilford and just kept walking. Andy explains that people have to learn to deal with sorrow, saying he learned it when Opie was "just a little bitty speck of a baby when I lost your ma just like you lost Wilford here." When Opie asks, "You did?" and Andy responds yes, Opie asks, "Who stepped on Ma?"

The pilot episode was an episode of *The Danny Thomas Show* filmed before a studio audience. Opie's line draws laughter from the audience before Andy explains he hadn't meant it in just that way. This accomplished establishing that Andy was a widower without being overly maudlin.

Andy promises Opie that when he gets home, he will take Opie to the creek and get a new turtle. Opie protests he doesn't want a new turtle; he wants Wilford. When Andy gently tells him he couldn't be that way, Opie innocently argues, "You didn't get a new Ma."

This scene also advances the story as Danny overhears the exchange from his cell and is moved. Seeing that Andy is more than the two-dimensional hayseed he had been treating him as, Danny speaks to him the first time as a real person, though of course, he ultimately still refuses to pay the fine.

The first time Andy's deceased wife was referenced in *The Andy Griffith Show* was on October 24, 1960, in "Ellie Comes to Town," the episode that introduced Ellie Walker as the first of Andy's love interests. Ellie meets Andy and Aunt Bee when she finds them in her uncle's drugstore and thinks they have broken in to commit a theft.

After Ellie learns the truth, Opie later comes by to see the new lady druggist in town. When Opie tells Ellie his name, she asks if he is any relation to Sheriff Taylor. He responds, "He's my Pa. Ain't got no Ma. But I got Aunt Bee. She takes care of me." After Andy enters and Ellie gives Opie a free ice cream cone on his earlier promise he won't say "ain't" anymore, Opie explains to Andy, "Didn't need any money, Pa. She's gonna' give it to me free just for not sayin' 'ain't' no more. So I ain't gonna' say 'ain't' no more." Opie then says, "She's a real nice lady, Pa, ain't she? I mean, isn't she?" When Andy agrees, Opie asks Ellie, "Are you married?" When she embarrassedly answers no, Opie adds, "My Pa ain't married either." Thus the path is cleared for a future romance.

Near the end of the second season, Opie's mother is mentioned one last time. In "Wedding Bells for Aunt Bee," Aunt Bee is under the mistaken impression that by living with Andy and Opie she is standing in the way of Andy finding a new mother for Opie. She allows clothes cleaner Fred Goss to court her even though she is not truly attracted to him. When Andy tells Opie the couple might marry, Opie asks why people get married. Andy answers the main reason is that they love each other. When Opie asks if Aunt Bee loving Mr. Goss means she doesn't love them anymore, Andy assures him it does not. Andy explains you can love a lot of people with the regular kind of love. "But then you meet that special person, and you got a special love all saved up for them. That's the marryin' kind of love, and that's the very best kind 'cause it comes from way down deep inside of your heart."

In a moving moment, Opie asks, "Did you and Mom have that deep-down kind?" Andy responds, "Yes, son, we did."

When was Andy first shown to be the Justice of the Peace?

The gag that Andy Taylor is both the Sheriff and the Justice of the Peace was in place from the beginning as shown in the pilot episode. In "Danny Meets Andy Griffith," entertainer Danny Williams is understandably upset when Andy removes a sign from his desk that reads "Sheriff" and replaces it with another that reads "Justice of the Peace."

In the ongoing series, while the show focuses on Andy as sheriff, literally the first shot of the character is a dissolve from the "Justice of the Peace" sign on the door to Andy in that role, performing the marriage of Rose and Wilbur Pine.

The first time Andy is shown to act as Justice of the Peace in a judicial capacity is in the third episode, "The Guitar Player" which first aired October 17, 1960, when Andy finds traveling bandleader Bobby Fleet guilty of a parking violation and fines him $20 or 24 hours in jail. This excessive punishment is really a ploy to trick Fleet into hearing Mayberry resident Jim Lindsey play the guitar in hopes he will hire him for his band.

The show often plays Andy's dual role for laughs. In the pilot episode, when Danny Williams first threatens that he will tell the justice of the peace what a bad police officer Andy is, Andy describes the Justice, saying, "Well, he's a fair-minded kind of a fella' and if he figures that I did wrong, why he'll probably tell me off pretty good." Legally, Williams would have had every right to be shocked that the arresting officer was also the judicial officer hearing the case. Likewise, Andy arresting Bobby Fleet on a trumped-up parking ticket citation and then imposing jail time would not be legal, even more so since Andy locked up the entire band who certainly all could not have co-owned the car and parked it.

The element of the desk sign switch used in the pilot is also sometimes used in the series. This is first seen after Barney arrested enough people to pack both jail cells while Andy was away for the day. As Andy calls the first case, instead of switching signs as he had in the pilot, he turns over his "Sheriff" sign to reveal the words "Justice of the Peace" printed on the other side.

The issue of the unfairness of such a situation arises again in "Andy and the Woman Speeder," an early second season episode. Journalist Elizabeth Crowley is caught speeding by Andy. She then rightfully complains that Andy being the arresting officer and also serving as Justice of the Peace is inherently unfair. Andy's response is to take her complaint as an unjust criticism of the court and hold her in contempt.

Griffith was not fond of the gag from the outset. As the series progressed, Andy is gradually seen less and less in the role of Justice of the Peace. Perhaps Griffith was bothered by the fact that Danny Williams and later Elizabeth Crowley were correct. One person holding both jobs in real life would be patently illegal and unjust. But as in all entertainment, the viewer must engage in a willing suspension of disbelief. Yes, one person could not legally serve in both roles. But Mayberry fans "let that go" in exchange for the joy the show brings. The series is not meant to be a documentary, but a presentation and celebration of small-town values for which so many yearn.

When was Andy first shown to carry a gun?

During the fifth season, Andy is the subject of an article titled "Sheriff Without a Gun" in *Law and Order*, a national magazine for sheriffs. The article is referenced again during the sixth season when a film with the same title was shot in Hollywood, allowing for a story arc in which the Taylors have an opportunity to visit California.

While Andy is known for not normally carrying a gun, he did do so upon occasion. The first time Andy is seen to carry a sidearm is in the second episode of the series, "Manhunt," which first aired on October 10, 1960. After Captain Barker and the State Police depart to set up roadblocks leaving Andy and Barney in the courthouse, Andy decides they will go out on their own to patrol side roads the State Police are clearly going to ignore. Preparing to leave, Andy takes his holster and gun out of the upper righthand drawer of his desk and straps the holster on.

Andy is shown to carry his revolver or a rifle several times. Six episodes after "Manhunt," Andy finds himself in the middle of a long-running feud between two mountain families, the Wakefields and the Carters, when two young people from the opposing families want to marry. After learning the families have been feuding and shooting at one another for 87 years without knowing why and in all that time there has not been a single fatality, Andy arranges a "duel" to be held between the two clan patriarchs. When he meets the two men to serve as "umpire" for the duel, Andy wears his own sidearm. After emptying their guns without their knowledge, he counts aloud their paces and then fires his revolver into the air causing both men to run away from one another without looking back.

Near the end of the same season, in "Barney Gets His Man," the deputy encounters escaped prisoner Eddie Brooke, unaware he is a fugitive. Barney tries to give Brooke a ticket for littering then accidentally becomes entangled with the escaped convict as Brooke tries to run from the State Police, resulting in Brooke's capture. The escaped convict vows revenge on Barney just before being taken away by the State Police. When Andy and Barney later learn Brooke has escaped again, they join the State Police in trying to recapture him. When they leave to join the search, Andy takes his holstered revolver and also removes a rifle from the gun rack.

Thus, out of the first 32 episodes of the initial season, Sheriff Andy Taylor was only shown to be armed three times. He would be armed even less often in future seasons.

Midway through the second season, Andy again wears a sidearm when he and Barney go to recapture escaped criminal Clarence Malloy. Five episodes later, Andy is again wearing his sidearm and carrying a rifle when he brings in the Gordon boys, moonshiners who ran a still in Franklin Hollow. Andy tells Barney his hand is bandaged because he had a difficult time bringing them in and they had stopped at Doc Zack's before coming to the cells. In reality, Andy Griffith's hand was bandaged because he had lost his temper and put his fist through a wall. These are the only two times Andy is shown armed that season.

During the third season, Andy is only shown armed once and it was in the final episode, "The Big House." As Andy is trying to stop four escapees from the Mayberry jail, his rifle is knocked out of his hand by temporary deputy Gomer who drops his own rifle from the courthouse rooftop. When Gomer then accidentally knocks over a bushel basket of light bulbs from the edge of the roof and the bulbs shatter on the sidewalk, the criminals think it is machine gunfire and surrender.

Andy again only carries a weapon in a single episode during the fourth season, arming himself to help guard the gold truck passing through town in "A Black Day for Mayberry." After this, he is never shown to be armed until one final time during the eighth and final season of *The Andy Griffith Show*. In "The Tape Recorder," when Andy receives a call from the State Police that they need him to hold a suspect on a bank robbery in Raleigh until the city detectives have a chance to question him, he takes a rifle from the gun rack as he leaves.

Andy's lack of normally being armed is the subject of the newly-elected Mayor Roy Stoner's first list of improvements he wants to see in the Mayberry Sheriff's Office. The irksome mayor complains to Andy that the situation is not what he calls good law enforcement. Andy responds, "Mayor, you know, over there in the old country—over there in London, England—them fellas over there, them policemen, they don't carry a gun at all. They just carry a stick. You want me and Barney to get a couple of sticks?"

Griffith later said the initial reason for this trait of the sheriff was, as an actor, he did not like the weight of a gun and holster on his hip and so preferred not to wear one on the show.

When did Andy first fire a gun?

Even though Andy occasionally is armed, he is shown to fire a gun while apprehending criminals only once.

The first time he is shown to fire a gun for any reason is during the "duel" he set up between the patriarchs of the feuding Wakefield and Carter clans in the episode "A Feud Is a Feud" which first aired December 5, 1960. Andy first says he needs to examine the rifles to be used in the duel but, in fact, empties them out of the eyesight of the men. (In a blooper, Andy accidentally switches the guns and hands the wrong ones back to each of the men.) Andy fires his own revolver into the air after only counting to two in order to scare the two men who both run when they hear the gunshot. One could argue Andy fires his gun here in the line of duty since he is trying to end the long-running feud, but he is really moved to do so in order to allow the young lovers Josh Wakefield and Hannah Carter to marry. Regardless, while he is not firing his weapon to apprehend a criminal, this was the first time he is shown to discharge his revolver.

Later in the first season, Andy again fires a gun in "Andy and the Gentleman Crook." Earlier in the episode, Barney accidentally fires his revolver in the courthouse. Andy reminds Barney he promised to keep his bullet in his shirt pocket. Barney responds, "Well, I'm sorry Andy. Doggone it, that bullet was turning green in my pocket. I thought it'd keep better in the gun. And besides, I've already lost two bullets in the laundry." Andy gives him one more bullet, making him promise to keep it in his shirt pocket and reminds him, "When you send that shirt to the laundry, unload." When well-known swindler and con man "Gentleman" Dan Caldwell is brought to be held in the jail, Barney loads his bullet into his gun without telling Andy. Later, Caldwell tricks Barney, gets his pistol, and ends up holding it on him to escape. Andy walks in to find Barney in the cell and Caldwell holding the gun on Aunt Bee and Opie who have also arrived. When the criminal points the gun at the sheriff, Andy asks where Caldwell got the gun and learns it is Barney's. Andy chuckles and assures Opie that Caldwell won't shoot him since there aren't any bullets in the gun. He tells Caldwell to go ahead and pull the trigger. Caldwell instead points it toward the ceiling and squeezes the trigger only to hear a click. He pulls the trigger four more times then meekly hands the gun over to Andy as he is placed back in the cell. Andy asks him, "Now, I ask you, Mr. Caldwell, what good would a gun do you that's as empty as this one?" He points the gun at the ceiling and fires. Andy is shocked to hear the gun go off and, realizing how close he came to being shot, has to sit down.

In the second season, in "The Perfect Female" Andy fires a rifle multiple times trying to impress Thelma Lou's cousin, Karen Moore, while shooting crows. (In another slight blooper, Thelma Lou first introduces her cousin as Karen Worth though her surname is Moore the rest of the episode.) Barney later tells Karen she has passed muster in Andy's eyes and answered all of Andy's questions just right, and tells her she is a lucky girl. The understandably irritated Karen registers to compete in a skeet shooting competition in which Andy is also entered. Unbeknownst to Andy, Karen is the skeet shooting champion of Arkansas. After Karen wins the contest, she gives Andy a taste of his own medicine, asking him multiple questions and saying she needed the answers to see if he could pass muster then walks away. Barney says, "Well, of all the unmitigated gall!" Andy replies he definitely had it and goes to apologize to Karen.

The only time Andy fires a gun while apprehending a criminal is midway through the sixth season in "Aunt Bee Takes a Job" which first aired on December 6, 1965. Aunt Bee has been hired by two counterfeiters who are pretending to run a printing shop as a front. When they realize their operation is about to be discovered, they try to make a quick getaway. Andy, who has deduced the truth, arrives just as they speed away. He grabs Deputy Warren Ferguson's gun and shoots out the tire, causing the clueless Aunt Bee to say, "I can't believe it. Just because they're going out of business is no reason to shoot at them!"

While it is not shown, in the third season episode, "High Noon in Mayberry, " it is revealed Andy had shot a man named Luke Comstock in the leg years earlier while stopping a gas station holdup. Comstock wrote a letter to Andy saying he was coming back to Mayberry to see him. While waiting for Comstock to arrive, Andy is concerned the man he had shot might have bad intentions. Andy takes a gun hidden on the top of the hutch in the dining area. He then decides not to keep the weapon and puts it back. Comstock does come bearing a shotgun, but it is a gift for Andy. Comstock explains that his injury had made him reconsider the path he was on. He turned his life around and now owns a chain of television repair stores in Cleveland, saying, "If you hadn't laid me up, who knows where I'd be today?"

When was Barney Fife first seen?

While Andy and Opie are first seen in the pilot episode for *The Andy Griffith Show*, "Danny Meets Andy Griffith," the episode does not include a deputy.

Don Knotts and Andy Griffith began a lifelong friendship while performing together in the hit Broadway play *No Time for Sergeants*. Griffith was reprising the lead role of Will Stockdale from an earlier version broadcast live as an episode of the television show *The United States Steel Hour*. Knotts was double cast in the Broadway version, playing both a preacher from Stockdale's hometown and a military officer administering a manual dexterity test. For the preacher's voice, Knotts used a character voice he had developed during his time on the radio serial *Bobby Benson and the B-Bar-B Riders* in which he played an "old timer" named Windy Wales. Griffith had listened to the radio show while traveling the South perfecting his comedy act. After Griffith heard Knotts' voice as the preacher, he asked him if he had played Windy Wales and was pleased to learn he was right. When Griffith later starred in the film version of *Sergeants*, Knotts reprised his role as the officer trying his best to administer the manual dexterity test to Stockdale.

On February 15, 1960, Knotts and his wife were playing cards at the home of Pat Harrington who years later would be widely known as handyman Schneider on the sitcom *One Day at a Time*. Both Knotts and Harrington were working on *The Steve Allen Show* but had recently learned the show had been canceled and would not be on the air much longer. Harrington had an upcoming guest appearance on *The Danny Thomas Show* and so wanted to watch the episode that night. Luckily for generations of future Mayberry fans, that was the night the pilot episode aired for what would become *The Andy Griffith Show*.

While Knotts and Griffith had not stayed in close touch after filming the hit movie *No Time for Sergeants*, Knotts immediately saw the potential of the pilot. The next day, he called Griffith and asked, "Listen, don't you think Sheriff Andy Taylor ought to have a deputy?"

A meeting was arranged for Knotts to meet with Sheldon Leonard to discuss the possible character. Leonard later said his original thought was Knotts would appear in just one or two episodes with the gag being he had been hired as a deputy because he was Andy's cousin. But after seeing the comic chemistry between the two, Knotts was soon offered a one-year contract to play Barney Fife with the agreement later replaced with a five-year contract.

As a friend of Griffith's, Knotts was allowed input into the character's name. Knotts suggested the last name "Fife" as a reference to a street he played on as a child, Fife Avenue in Morgantown, West Virginia, Knotts' hometown.

The first episode of *The Andy Griffith Show* was directed by Sheldon Leonard. As noted earlier, Andy was the first character seen clearly and as the camera pulled out, Opie was the second. The third whose face could be seen clearly was Barney.

When was Aunt Bee first seen?

Aunt Bee is not seen in the pilot episode though Frances Bavier, the actress who played her, is. In the pilot, Andy refers to being helped at home by his Aunt Lucy, a character who is not shown. Bavier instead plays Henrietta Perkins in the pilot. Henrietta is behind on her taxes because she has been paying hand-me-down shop owner Mr. Johnson for the rental of a suit. When her husband died, she rented the suit for him to be displayed in during the funeral but forgot to tell the undertaker to remove it before the burial. Johnson has been charging her 50 cents a day rental for two years amounting to over $350 for a suit that only cost $50 brand new. Andy later reasons one could argue she was buying the suit on a lay-away plan.

The first episode of *The Andy Griffith Show*, "The New Housekeeper," aired on October 3, 1960. The character of Aunt Bee is introduced when she comes to take the place of the previous housekeeper, Rose. One might assume she is first seen when Andy opens the front door but it is possible to argue that she is actually seen just a few moments before, albeit in the form of a picture. As Andy is speaking to Opie before answering the door, a picture of what could be a young woman is seen on the wall behind them.

In the 1994 book *Inside Mayberry*, the authors stated the picture was of a young Bavier in her ingenue days. However, it has since been verified that the picture is actually a print of an oil painting titled "Child with an Apple" completed in the late 1700s by the French painter Jean-Baptiste Greuze.

One of the authors of *Inside Mayberry* has since stated he cannot recall which cast or crew member or producer told him the picture was a young Bavier. So it may be he was told the picture was *intended* to represent a young Aunt Bee and the author misunderstood, believing it an actual picture of her. Regardless, the image is definitely not of a young Bavier.

The picture actually appears several times early in the series. It occasionally moves slightly during the first season, though these small changes in position were likely simply the result of the set being dressed in different ways, as initially the picture hangs above a chair but later hangs above a bookcase on the same wall. In the picture's final appearance in the second season episode "Aunt Bee's Brief Encounter," the picture now hangs beside the front door. Don Knotts once explained that story consultant Aaron Ruben often changed or shifted pictures on the set for unknown reasons.

While Aunt Bee is first seen in the series premiere, she was nearly not seen until the second episode. The producers initially strongly considered using "Manhunt" as the inaugural representation of Mayberry. "Manhunt" has the advantage of showing the rural attitudes of Andy overcoming the big city attitudes of the out-of-town State Police, a theme that recurred often over the life of the series. Aunt Bee does appear in "Manhunt," but her brief appearance could easily have been removed as it is not integral to the story. However, the show's sponsors insisted that the heart-warming story of Opie learning to accept Aunt Bee be the first episode. Afterward, the producers made the decision to always have the first episode every season be one centered on Opie.

When was the first reference to Aunt Bee's name actually being "Beatrice?"

The name of the character of Aunt Bee often confuses newer or more casual fans who understandably assume it is spelled "Bea" as a shortened version of "Beatrice." Aunt Bee's actual name was indeed Beatrice, but when was this first seen?

The character is called Aunt Bee by most, though some of her peers such as Clara and Fred Goss sometimes call her simply "Bee." The correct spelling in the show is clearly "Bee" which presumably is a nickname. Frances Bavier was listed as playing Aunt "Bee" in the scripts themselves, the occasional episode title (the first being the December 4, 1961 episode "Aunt Bee's Brief Encounter"), and public releases of information such as *TV Guide* listings. After Don Knotts left the series as a regular cast member, Bavier's name was added to the opening credits with her character's name of Aunt Bee listed as well. In the seventh season episode "Aunt Bee's Restaurant," the spelling of her nickname is shown in the window of her new business venture which was called "Aunt Bee's Canton Palace."

Aunt Bee's actual name is eventually stated to be Beatrice, though not until the fifth season. On October 5, 1964, in "Family Visit," the third episode of Season 5, when Nora and Ollie first arrive, Nora yells as she is coming up the stairs, "Hello, Beatrice!" Two episodes later, on October 19, 1964, in "Aunt Bee's Romance" Bee receives a letter. Since the envelope has a smudged return address, she spends some time trying to guess who it could be from. As she examines the letter, viewers can see it is addressed to "Miss Beatrice Taylor." Though it aired two episodes later, "Aunt Bee's Romance" was actually filmed the week right after "Family

Visit." After four full seasons of Aunt Bee's given name not being stated, it finally was in two episodes in a row.

In the eighth season episode "Aunt Bee and the Lecturer," visiting speaker Hubert St. John is clearly smitten with Aunt Bee when he is introduced. Presumably, he would not have been aware of the unusual spelling Aunt Bee uses. He asks, "Bea. That's the diminutive for Beatrice, isn't it?" Aunt Bee confirmed her actual name was Beatrice when she responded, "Oh, well, I haven't been called Beatrice since I was a little girl."

Interestingly, Bavier typically signed autographs and added her character's name with the traditional spelling of "Bea." However, her cemetery marker bears the correct spelling of her most famous character's name.

When was Andy first underestimated by a city slicker?

The recurring motif of the small town country sheriff actually being wiser than an arrogant city person who looks down on him is part of *The Andy Griffith Show* from the outset.

In *The Danny Thomas Show*, Thomas plays Danny Williams, a New York nightclub entertainer and comedian. In the Mayberry pilot episode "Danny Meets Andy Griffith," Danny is brought to the courthouse after being stopped by Sheriff Taylor. The humor in this episode is broad and not the more sophisticated approach that would eventually be seen in *The Andy Griffith Show*. Danny was stopped for a stop sign violation but is upset since the stop sign was along a road where there was no intersection. Andy explains, "Well, now, the town council did vote to put a road in there, about, oh, I believe it was about six years ago, I believe it was. The only trouble is, so far we just raised enough money for the stop sign."

When Andy as Justice of the Peace is ready to impose the standard fine of $5, Danny pulls a large roll of cash out of his pocket. When Andy says it is sometimes a $10 fine, Danny lays the $10 down and says, "Be my guest. Ten. Big deal." He then throws down an extra $5 and adds, "Go buy yourself a comb and rake the hayseed out of your hair."

Realizing the normal fine will mean nothing to Danny, Andy raises it to $100 or 10 days in jail which Danny refuses to pay, instead choosing to serve the jail time.

At first, Danny treats Andy poorly, calling him a crooked politician and mocking his Southern accent. He ultimately tries to embarrass Andy during a national television interview. When Andy admits to the interviewer that he did increase the fine, he explains that the regular fine could not have meant less to Danny so he had to increase the fine so Danny would feel the weight of the law. He adds that a famous entertainer like Danny influences people who admire him and might follow the example he sets. "So the way I see it, a big man has got more of a responsibility to obey the law and respect the folks who enforce it, even though they might be what he calls rubes and hicks." When the interviewer asks if Danny called him by those names, Andy says, "Sometimes. Then other times he was downright rude." Realizing Andy is right and that he has behaved poorly, Danny admits he has been wrong and apologizes to Andy during the broadcast "for being a virulent city slicker."

This storyline of a big city or authoritarian figure looking down on Andy as a small town sheriff but then getting their comeuppance became a recurring theme in *The Andy Griffith Show*. In fact, in only the second episode, "Manhunt," which first aired on October 10, 1960, Andy has to deal with Captain Barker of the State Police. When Andy first offers to help in any way he can, Barker ignores him and has one of his men set up a metal map of the area with magnets to show where roadblocks should be placed. Andy says, "Well, now, that's a nice, shiny new map there but it ain't much different than the one we had up there before." He then points out that Barker's plan to guard the main roads is fine so long as the escaped criminal they are searching for is taking the bus. Barker ignores his advice and leaves with his officers to set up the roadblocks, telling Andy and Barney to stay at the jail and take care of their local affairs. In the course of the episode, at one point Barker angrily tells Andy, "Sheriff, we're trying to apprehend a dangerous criminal. Please don't hinder us with your bumbling ideas!"

At the end of the episode, Andy uses common sense "smarts" and tricks the criminal into trying to escape across a lake in a rowboat that Andy knows will sink due to a leak in the boat. This results in the capture of the criminal without any shots needing to be fired. Barker realizes he has been wrong. When Opie later says his pa is the best sheriff in the whole state, Barker says, "Wouldn't be surprised, son."

"Captain, if you'll take your men down this little road down there at the shore, I imagine he'll swim right to you."

Barker was played by Ken Lynch who played the same character type four different times in *The Andy Griffith Show*. In the episode, "Jailbreak," he is with the State Bureau of Investigation and asks Andy to stay out of their way, saying, "I suppose you've got plenty of other things to keep you busy. Chicken thieves and whatnot." (He later plays a Treasury agent escorting a gold truck through Mayberry and Inspector Rogers of the Highway Patrol concerned Andy cannot handle his duties as sheriff while also running a laundromat.)

The greatest problem caused by a "big city" troublemaker is seen in "Andy on Trial." Newspaper publisher J. Howard

Jackson is given a speeding ticket which he says he will come back to Mayberry to resolve and then fails to do so. When Andy comes to the large city and is seated in Jackson's palatial office, Jackson says, "You really are a conscientious sheriff, aren't you? I would imagine you'd have your hands full way out there in Mayberry running down chicken thieves and curfew breakers." When Jackson says he cannot come with Andy immediately for a trial and says he is sure they can settle the matter, he reaches inside his jacket presumably for his wallet, Andy says, "I hope you're reachin' for a comb or a handkerchief or something, 'cause we take a very dim view of bribery in Mayberry. Bribery's one of the things we like to watch on account of there ain't much else to do."

After being arrested and escorted back to Mayberry then found guilty and fined $15, Jackson is incensed. He tells his attorney who he had arranged to meet him there, "Oh, boy, these hicks. They sure love to go after the big game, don't they?" Jackson has one of his reporters pose as a college journalism student to gather information to be presented in the least favorable light, then publishes an article alleging malfeasance by Andy. As a result, the State Attorney's Office brings charges against Andy and suspends him from office pending a hearing. But after the facts are made clear in a moving speech by Barney from the witness stand and with the only evidence being the misleading article, the commissioner conducting the hearing dismisses the case and apologizes to Andy for any inconvenience or embarrassment caused.

When was Barney's first love interest seen?

When fans think of Barney's love life, they first think of the adorable Thelma Lou, but there were earlier girlfriends for Barney. The first is the shy Miss Rosemary who appears in only one episode, "Andy the Matchmaker" which first aired on November 14, 1960. Being only the seventh episode in the first season, the stronger Southern accents and less delineated characters seen early in the series are on full display. Barney eventually evolves to one who thought himself quite the ladies' man, but he is painfully shy in this early episode.

Miss Rosemary.

Rosemary is a seamstress who has lengthened the sleeves of Andy's "judgin' coat" an inch. When Andy learns Barney has been walking Rosemary to preaching every Sunday, he knows that Barney is sweet on her. But Barney's self-esteem is at a low after reading a poem some children had written about him in chalk on the side of the bank. He feels that since there are no big crimes to solve, people view him as a nobody. Rosemary is as shy as Barney which makes Andy's attempts to get them together difficult. When Andy tells Rosemary she could have her pick of a dozen men in Mayberry, she says Andy is "putting her on" and adds, "Nobody'd want me."

In order to build up Barney's view of himself, Andy and Ellie stage a fake drugstore robbery, giving the gleeful Barney the opportunity to try to dust for fingerprints (though after making a mess with the powder, he decides the criminal was probably wearing gloves anyway). Barney soon apprehends the criminal who he believes committed the non-existent crime. Luckily, the man he caught actually was wanted on five other charges in Chattanooga.

Once the story hits the front page, Barney starts to exhibit the bravado he would later often show, saying he has not asked Miss Rosemary on a date as he figures he shouldn't limit himself now that he is well known. However, his shyness returns as soon as he is in her presence. Thanks to Andy's intervention, a date is finally made with

Barney and Miss Rosemary shaking hands on the deal.

This episode includes Barney referring to himself as a "trained noticer," a descriptive phrase that has been adopted by the Mayberry community to mean a fan who notices small, easy-to-miss aspects of an episode such as bloopers. The episode also includes a mention by Andy of Snappy Lunch, an actual restaurant in his hometown of Mount Airy, North Carolina that is still in business. Andy suggests to Barney, "You wanna' double date? I'm gonna' take Miss Ellie to the picture show Saturday night. You and Miss Rosemary can go with us and then after the show, why, we can go down to Snappy Lunch and get somethin' to eat and some coffee. Want to?"

Barney did have one other love interest before Thelma Lou. Hilda Mae was first seen in "Ellie for Council," aired on December 12, 1960. On a picnic by the lake, it seems clear Barney, who had been painfully shy with Miss Rosemary, must have been seeing Hilda Mae for a while since he is not shy around her. When they decide to take a walk in the woods, after struggling to help her stand up, Barney tells Hilda Mae it is not the wild animals she should be worried about. Hilda Mae appears only one other time but was also referred to in "Christmas Story" when she sends Barney a Christmas card in which she calls him "Barney Parney Pooh."

Hilda Mae.

When did Andy first act to protect Barney's ego?

Another recurring theme seen often in *The Andy Griffith Show* is Andy acting to protect Barney's fragile ego. The first instance of this behavior is shown in "Andy Saves Barney's Morale," originally broadcast on February 20, 1961. In the episode, Andy leaves Barney in charge as Acting Sheriff while he is away for the day in Centerville to testify. When Andy returns eight hours later, he discovers that Barney has people locked in the two cells packed "like sardines in a can." As citizens are let out of the cells, Andy is particularly surprised to see Franklin from the bank, Mayor Pike, and Aunt Bee with Opie in tow.

As Justice of the Peace, Andy hears and dismisses all 19 cases. Barney instantly becomes the butt of jokes by townspeople. When Barney comes into the barbershop, Mayor Pike calls him "Wild Bill" Fife. Barney soon feels he has become a laughingstock in town and shows up for work the next day unshaven, his collar unbuttoned, his tie askew, and his pants wrinkled because he has slept in them. Andy later learns that Hilda Mae has already tried to buttress Barney's ego. Discussing her date with Barney the previous night, she says, "Sheriff, I tell ya', I buttered that fella up frontways, backways, sideways, and edgewise." She paid him numerous compliments and sat bent over so he would feel taller. "I tell ya', Sheriff, that fella was so buttered up if you tried to grab him, he'd squoosh right of your hand." Unfortunately, she found herself unable to control her laughter after she ran her fingers through his hair and it stood in all directions.

To save Barney's morale, Andy begins letting it be known

throughout town and at home to Aunt Bee that he plans to fire Barney as he cannot have a deputy at whom people are laughing. Soon, those who had been arrested come back to the jail and walk into the cells, saying in front of Andy and Barney they are guilty and are glad the deputy showed no favoritism in enforcing the law.

The theme recurs in various forms throughout the rest of Barney's time on the show. Ten episodes later, Barney accidentally apprehends escaped convict Eddie Brooke who then threatens revenge in "Barney Gets His Man." After Brooke escapes from the State Troopers who took custody after Barney's "capture," he heads back to Mayberry in a stolen car. When the car is discovered abandoned outside of town, an obviously frightened Barney overcomes his fear and goes with Andy to help the two troopers try to recapture Brooke. When Andy realizes Brooke is hiding in a hayloft, he has Barney wait in the barn knowing Brooke will make his move. Andy then hides outside where he can see into the interior through loose boards on the wall. When Brooke comes down the ladder to attack the unsuspecting Barney, Andy throws a rock to knock over a can. The startled Barney jumps up and fires his weapon wildly which causes Brooke to immediately surrender, saying he doesn't have a gun. The State Troopers come in and naturally assume Barney has singlehandedly captured Brooke again.

There are many other examples. In "Barney's Replacement," Andy tricks Barney into rejoining the sheriff's department after Barney has been selling vacuum cleaners door-to-door. Andy does so by demonstrating that the state attorney working as a temporary deputy relies too much on statistics and not enough on the human element needed for the job. In "Sheriff Barney," after Andy and Barney switch jobs for the day so Barney can get a taste of what it is like to be sheriff since he has been offered that position in the town of Greendale, Barney realizes he is not capable. In order to restore Barney's confidence, when moonshiner Rafe Hollister tries to turn himself in, Andy has Rafe find Barney and surrender to him instead. Rafe has a hard time doing so as Barney keeps rebuffing him and telling him to pester someone else, but Rafe eventually succeeds. In "The Big House," Andy lets the two plainclothes officers from Memphis think the use of breaking lightbulbs to simulate gunfire from a machine gun was part of a plan by Barney.

Even after Don Knotts left the show, the theme is used in two of Knotts' five guest appearances in the show. The last time it was utilized is in the color episode "A Visit to Barney Fife" which involves a string of grocery store robberies carried out by a family who also rent Barney a room, enabling them to use information Barney carelessly gives to avoid being caught. Barney is on the verge of being fired but Andy's intervention allows him to get the credit for solving the case and keep his job.

Of course, Andy does not only protect Barney's ego in work matters. In "The Clubmen," to spare Barney's feelings, Andy allows Barney to believe it is Andy who was not asked to join The Esquire Club. In "Barney and the Cave Rescue," after a cave collapse, Andy and Helen re-enter the cave from which they had already escaped so Barney will be a hero. In "Back to Nature," Gomer helps Andy convince Opie and his friends that Barney is an expert outdoorsman. In perhaps the fan-favorite example, Andy prevents Barney from being removed from the choir by convincing him his solo must be sung silently into an incredibly sensitive microphone and then having another singer perform the part from backstage in "Barney and the Choir."

When was Mayor Pike first seen?

The first mayor shown in Mayberry is Mayor Pike. His introduction is part of a visual gag when Barney is manning a roadblock on a backroad near Mayberry in "Manhunt," which originally aired October 10, 1960 as the second episode of the series. Barney insists on frisking everyone he stops, just in case they are the criminal being searched for wearing a disguise. After frisking a short, rotund man, Barney says, "All right. I guess that'll do it. Be sure and say hello to the little woman, Mayor."

Mayor Pike was played by character actor Dick Elliott who stood five feet, four inches tall and spoke in a distinctive high-pitched voice with a sibilant "s." Elliott's portrayal made Mayor Pike a popular recurring character early in the series. The character's surname was inspired by Floyd Pike, a businessman Andy knew in Mount Airy, North Carolina who founded the Pike Electric Company.

The mayor is easily swayed though he is unaware of this trait. In "Mayberry Goes Hollywood," after filmmaker Mr. Harmon makes a presentation to the town council about his desire to make a movie in Mayberry and then is excused, Mayor Pike immediately says he does not like the idea. But when Andy says a motion picture being made in Mayberry might be good for the town, Pike agrees and says, "Well, that's just what I've been thinking. Might be a good thing for the town." When the council members then express concern the outsider might be planning to make fun of the way people in Mayberry talk or look, perhaps even making fun of their "little fat mayor," Mayor Pike switches sides again. Rather than be offended by the remark, Mayor Pike asks Andy, "Are you going to allow that, Andy? Are you going to let them make a picture here and laugh at your fat little mayor?" After Andy suggests he be allowed to take Mr. Harmon on a tour of the town to learn his intentions, Mayor Pike is still strongly opposed until he hears the council members agree it is a good idea, at which point he switches sides yet again and tells everyone, "I'm so glad you all see it my way." Andy replies, "Well, now that's what makes you such a good mayor. You think for yourself."

The mayor is always quick to have his family members perform at public events. After Mr. Harmon is given the go-ahead to make the film, when he arrives with his crew, the welcoming ceremony includes Pike's daughter, Juanita (No, not *that* Juanita!) singing a verse of Scottish poet Robert Burns' "Flow Gently, Sweet Afton." Later in the season, both when a plaque is to be presented to the descendant of Revolutionary War hero Nathan Tibbs and when a welcoming celebration is planned for the return of hometown guitarist Jim Lindsey, Mayor Pike again suggests Juanita sing. The mayor's wife also liked to perform, traditionally singing opera while riding a horse as the grand finale of the town's Founder's Day celebration.

Juanita Pike was played by Josie Lloyd who would appear in later seasons as the recurring character Lydia Crosswaithe. Lloyd also played Josephine Pike, the mayor's daughter who vied for the title of "Miss Mayberry." Since Lloyd played the roles in both episodes, they likely were meant to be the same character with a different first name accidentally used.

Mayor Pike appears in seven episodes during the first season and four more during the first half of the second. His last appearance was in "The Manicurist." Dick Elliott passed away on December 22, 1961, exactly one month before the "The Manicurist" originally aired.

When were Barney's parents first seen or referenced?

The first time one of Barney's parents is referenced is also the only time one was actually seen. In the second episode "Manhunt," when Barney is left to man a roadblock on a backroad near Mayberry, he insists on frisking everyone he stops in case they are the criminal in disguise. After frisking a man he knew named Cal and then Mayor Pike, he frisks a plump woman and tells her he is sorry but they can't take chances. She then turns around and says, "But Barney, I'm your mother!"

The inclusion of Barney's mother in this early episode was obviously intended simply as a great visual joke, but as *The Andy Griffith Show* continued, references to Barney being like his mother came to be a running gag. The first instance of this is in "A Plaque for Mayberry" which originally aired on April 3, 1961. After learning a descendant of a Revolutionary War hero lives in Mayberry whose identity is being sought, Barney suggests he might be the descendant. When Andy is amused at the thought, Barney is offended. Andy says he is sorry and that he didn't know Barney would be so sensitive about it. Barney responds, "Well, I am. I'm very sensitive. I'm like my mother. She's very sensitive. All us Fifes are sensitive."

Three episodes later, Barney tries to keep Andy from looking at a filled citation pad by putting the pad under his cap. He was trying to hide that he had written some personal information in the pad about a certain new waitress working at the Junction Cafe. When Andy playfully tries to grab Barney's cap from his head, Barney says he doesn't like people touching his hat. "I'm like my mother. She don't like people touching her hat either." Andy laughs, then explains, "I was just picturing you and your mother sittin' around the house with your hats pulled down over your ears." Barney is defensive of his mother, finally letting Andy see the citation pad while adding, "But you leave my mother out of this."

Barney's father is not mentioned as often but is referenced a few times. He is first mentioned in the third season episode "Class Reunion," originally aired on February 4, 1963. When Andy and Barney are storing a trunk owned by the deputy in Andy's garage, Andy finds a rock among the contents. In a bittersweet exchange, when Barney tells him the rock was his father's, Andy says he was sorry, making it clear that Barney's father has passed away. Barney tells him not to feel sad as there is a lot of happiness connected to the rock which his dad used to keep on his desk. Barney says, "I used to strike kitchen matches on it and hold 'em to daddy's pipe. Ya' know, for a little fella it was a big kick to strike a match and hold it to your dad's pipe."

Two episodes later his father is mentioned again. In "Opie and the Spoiled Kid," Barney says as a child he was never spanked, explaining his father couldn't since Barney was a lot bigger than him. Andy says, "I thought as a child you were sickly." Barney responds, "Well, he was sicklier."

However, six episodes later, Barney and Andy are sitting on the Taylor front porch. Planning to buy a car, Barney tells Andy the purchase will be about the biggest he has ever made. He adds, "Last big buy I made was my mom's and dad's anniversary present." When Andy asks what he got them, Barney answers a septic tank. Barney adds, "Oh, they're really hard to buy for." His use of the present tense made it clear his parents were both still alive. The inconsistency of whether Barney's father was still alive or had passed away also applied to his mother.

In the next-to-last episode of the third season, Andy has to introduce Barney to the Darlings, recalling that Barney had not met them the first time they were in town since he had taken his mother on a bus trip to Charlotte. The obvious implication is that Barney's mother is still alive.

In "The Sermon for Today," only the fourth episode of the next season, Barney's mother has evidently passed away. Discussing the large meal they had just had after church, Barney says, "Fortunately, none of mine goes to fat. It all goes to muscle. That's a mark of us Fifes. Everything we eat goes to muscle." He adds, referring to his mother in the past tense, "My mother was the same way. She could just eat and eat and eat and eat and eat." But seven episodes later, Barney is again referring to his mother as still being alive. When he explains his dedication to his duty after issuing Gomer a ticket, he speaks in the present tense, saying, "If my mother made a U-turn, I'd give her a ticket." Yet five episodes later, Barney again refers to his mother in the past tense when Andy puts on Barney's motorcycle helmet in "Barney's Sidecar." When Andy jokingly asks how he looks wearing the helmet, Barney tersely says, "Don't wear my hat, Ange." When Andy says he was just trying it on, Barney says, "I can't stand to wear a hat after it's been on somebody else's head. My mother was the same way. She just couldn't stand to wear a hat after it'd of been on somebody else's head." Andy responds he remembers that about Barney's mother.

At the end of the fourth season, Barney's mother was again referred to in the past tense, though it did not seem as clear she was not still alive. While impatiently waiting for Aunt Bee to arrive at the courthouse with lunch, Barney tells Andy he has a clock in his stomach that tells him when it was time for meals. "I go by that clock, too. Tick, tick. I know it's time for lunch. Tick, tick. I know it's time for dinner. My mother was the same way." Andy again says he remembers that about his mother. This certainly sounds as if she has died. But Andy then uses the past tense when referring to the clock in Barney's stomach. When Barney says his mother had a clock in her stomach, Andy asks, "Hey, Barn? These clocks you and your mother had in your stomach—Did the tickin' keep your father awake at night?" It appears Andy was just being loose with his use of tense since Barney had used the present tense in saying he has—not had—a clock in his stomach. While not completely clear, it also seems Barney's mother is still alive when Barney defends her against Andy's ribbing. After Barney warns Andy not to get facetious (though mispronouncing the word), Andy says he was just kidding and Barney says, "I don't mind you kiddin' me about my stomach, but don't kid about my mother's stomach!"

Other examples include Barney being superstitious like his mother (though he insisted he and his mother were not superstitious, they were just cautious), sanitary like his mother, and neat like his mother. In all of these instances, his mother is referred to in the past tense.

In addition to the inconsistency of whether Barney's parents were still alive or had passed away, there is another inconsistency regarding his mother's physical build.

As noted, in "The Sermon for Today," Barney's describes his mother as having been able to eat and eat yet still be thin. This matched another reference he makes to her in the earlier episode "Class Reunion" where it is clear his father has died. In addition to his daddy's rock, Barney also has a copy of his and Andy's high school yearbook. When Barney sees his high school picture, he comments that he was painfully thin back then. He says, "Well, I got my mother's family's frame. When I was 17, I could reach into a milk bottle and take out an egg." (Barney fails to offer an explanation of just why an egg would be in a milk bottle.) These descriptions of his mother as thin obviously contradict the only time Barney's mother is actually shown in "Manhunt" where she is plump.

The producers were far more concerned in telling a good story than in strict continuity. In addition, they could not have foreseen the ready availability of digital formats that make it easier for "trained noticers" to watch for such continuity errors. These inconsistencies definitely do not diminish the overall wonderful storytelling involved.

Others of Barney's family are mentioned only briefly. His grandmother is mentioned once when Barney is reading a book of hers titled *Signs, Omens, Portents, and Charms to Ward Off Bad Luck*. An uncle is mentioned in Knotts' final appearance as Barney Fife as a series regular. Barney, Andy, and Aunt Bee are discussing college. Barney says, "Well, I blew my chance at the big ball o' wax right in high school. My mind wandered." When Andy asks where his mind had wandered, Barney admits to girls mostly. Barney thinks it is unfortunate, explaining, "I had a good connection, too. The FBI. Yeah, a direct line. My uncle knew a man who used to do a lot of their plumbing in Washington."

When was Andy first shown to play a musical instrument?

Music played an important role in Andy Griffith's life so it is not surprising that music also played an important role in his show. As a child growing up in Mount Airy, North Carolina, Griffith was exposed to the guitar at an early age. His mother played the musical instrument publicly, performing at informal local dance parties.

Griffith was also a fan of swing music he heard on the radio and dreamed of becoming a musician. When he was 14, he saw the 1941 Bing Crosby film *Birth of the Blues* and was enthralled with the trombone playing of Jack Teagarden. Often called the "Father of Jazz Trombone," Teagarden was renowned as a jazz trombonist, bandleader, composer, and singer. Twenty years later, Griffith had the opportunity to provide Teagarden with what turned out to be his last acting role. In *The Andy Griffith Show*, the famous trombonist played one of the councilmen in Greendale who thought Barney would make a good sheriff in "Sheriff Barney" which first aired Christmas Day, 1961.

Griffith's viewing of *Birth of the Blues* made him determined to learn to play the trombone himself. He lied about his age to get a job with the National Youth Administration to sweep at his school. He saved the $6 a month he was paid until he had enough to order a trombone from a Spiegel catalog. The local Moravian Church minister Ed Mickey gave Griffith lessons and he became proficient enough on the instrument that he was soon playing solos.

While Andy Taylor never plays the trombone in the series,

in "The Sermon for the Day," he plays the tuba when a futile attempt is made to resurrect the Mayberry town band for a concert under the stars. However, the first instrument Andy plays in the series and the one played most frequently is the acoustic guitar.

Andy is first seen playing guitar in the October 3, 1960 episode "The New Housekeeper," the first episode of the series, when he is shown playing on the front porch of his house in the closing scene. The guitar was definitely the sheriff's instrument of choice. One need only look at the first season to see it would be a prevalent sight on the show to see Andy playing. He was shown playing the guitar on his front porch four more times in the first season alone.

Of course, Andy also kept a "stringed instrument" on hand at the courthouse. He first plays there while accompanying Jim Lindsey in the third episode, "The Guitar Player," and uses it later in the episode to trick Jim into playing for Bobby Fleet. Andy plays the guitar in the courthouse three more times during the first season.

When one adds when Andy plays guitar at a picnic by the lake in "Ellie for Council" (though he isn't actually shown playing it in the episode), at Floyd's when playing for Mr. Maxwell in "Mayberry on Record," at Ellie's house in "Cyrano Andy," and at Sam Becker's house for a hastily organized baby shower in "Quiet Sam," Andy plays guitar twelve times during the show's inaugural season, or in more than a third of the episodes. The sheriff continues to play the guitar throughout the entire series.

The first three times Andy is shown playing guitar, his instrument has the traditional pickguard below the opening in the body. Beginning with the tenth episode, "Ellie for

Council," Andy more often plays a guitar that is missing a pickguard. That guitar was a Martin he had first played in the 1957 film *A Face in the Crowd* directed by Elia Kazan. In the film, Griffith plays "Lonesome" Rhodes, a corrupt Arkansas guitar player who becomes a media star while being disdainful of his fans. The film prop department obtained a new Martin D-18, painted it black, then glued sequins on the body to spell out "Lonesome" and "Momma."

After filming, Griffith was able to keep the guitar. He removed the sequins and the pickguard and spent nine days sanding the paint off the body. He then had the guitar professionally refinished and chose not to replace the pickguard. The guitar became his favorite and he began using it on *The Andy Griffith Show* as well.

When was someone other than Andy playing a guitar first seen?

While Andy Taylor plays the guitar often beginning with the premier episode of *The Andy Griffith Show*, the instrument is also played by others during the series.

Mayberry resident Jim Lindsey is the first person shown to play after Andy did so. In the third episode of the series, "The Guitar Player," originally aired October 17, 1960, Orville Monroe complains to Andy that Jim is disturbing the peace, playing on the sidewalk in front of Monroe's Funeral Parlor and Mortuary with a crowd gathered around listening appreciatively. During the course of the episode, Andy arrests both the leader and all the members of a band passing through town called Bobby Fleet and His Band with a Beat in order to have Fleet hear Lindsey play. After the band is jailed, Jim is brought in on a trumped-up charge. While he initially refuses to play for Fleet, he does agree to tune Andy's acoustic guitar. As he does so and the band members taunt him, he begins playing. The emotion of the scene allows the viewer to overlook that what is actually heard is an electric guitar. Jim is hired on the spot to join Fleet's band.

Jim Lindsey was played by James Best who was asked whether he could play the guitar before being offered the part. He later recalled he enthusiastically responded that he owned two guitars, which was true. He neglected to mention that he could not play them. In close-ups of the guitar being played, they are clearly not Best's hands.

Jim returns near the end of the first season, having quit the band and pretending to be besieged with offers to perform when he actually has no money or gigs. Jim brags he owns three guitars. Andy soon realizes what has happened and arrests Jim on another trumped-up charge after having arranged for Fleet to return to Mayberry to bail Jim out of jail. Fleet does so while also giving the guitarist a raise resulting in Jim again leaving Mayberry never to be seen again.

Others were shown to play guitar, but several are of particular note. Later in the first season in "Mayberry on Record," independent record producer Mr. Maxwell comes to town to record music for an album. He records Andy playing with an unnamed group of musicians, one of who played the guitar and another who played a resonator guitar, often called a dobro. ("Dobro" is actually a brand name currently owned by the Gibson Guitar Corporation.) All but one of the band are seen again 10 episodes later in "Quiet Sam" as part of an impromptu celebration of the new baby born to Sam and Lily Becker. The unnamed band members were played by the bluegrass band The Country Boys. The guitarist was Clarence White who later joined The Byrds after Gram Parsons left the group. He was tragically killed by a drunk driver at the age of 29. The dobro guitarist was LeRoy McNees who is still an active performer under the stage name LeRoy Mack. The songs The Country Boys played on the show were later included on the album *Songs, Themes & Laughs From The Andy Griffith Show*. Shortly after their appearances in Mayberry, the talented band renamed themselves The Kentucky Colonels. The band was inducted into the International Bluegrass Music Hall of Fame in 2019.

During the third season, another group of musicians was needed to play a group of mountain men who were the sons of Briscoe Darling. The Darling brothers were played by the now-legendary bluegrass band The Dillards with Rodney Dillard playing the guitar. The Darling boys appeared in half a dozen episodes, always performing their bluegrass wizardry. The Dillards became pioneers in what is now called the "Newgrass" movement of the early 1960s, a movement which included electric instruments. As such, they were highly influential on what became the country rock genre.

During the color years, the guitar features prominently in two episodes. In the second episode of the first color season, Andy becomes jealous of Frank Smith, a member of the Raleigh School Board who is in town for a couple of weeks to work on a project with Helen. Frank seems to be an expert at everything, causing Aunt Bee to continually try to convince Andy to call attention to his own abilities. When Andy, Helen, and Frank go outside to sit on the front porch after dinner, Aunt Bee brings out Andy's guitar and asks him to play, telling Frank that Andy plays beautifully. (The guitar was not Griffith's favorite guitar that was missing a pickguard.) When Helen reminds Frank he had mentioned he plays guitar, he says it has been a long time. Andy hands him the guitar and Frank again implies they should not expect much, then proceeds to expertly play a flamenco number with blindingly fast fingering, causing Helen to comment, "Oh, Frank, you're wonderful!"

During the final color season, Opie is invited to join the local teenage rock band The Sound Committee as a guitarist. After bandleader Clifford asks him to work on not talking like a kid, Opie immediately begins refining his image, telling Clifford during a break, "I think I'll split over there and get some of those cool-looking potato chips."

When was Barney first shown to play a musical instrument?

Barney was seen to play three musical instruments in *The Andy Griffith Show*, but undoubtedly his instrument of choice was one he sometimes carried with him: the harmonica.

Barney plays the harmonica in the first scene of the inaugural episode, "The New Housekeeper" aired October 3, 1960. The opening scene of the series shows Andy as Justice of the Peace marrying Rose, his and Opie's former housekeeper, to Wilbur Pines. Barney plays "Here Comes the Bride" on the harmonica at the wedding.

Barney's playing is shown several times during the first season. In "Those Gossipin' Men," a traveling shoe salesman named Wilbur Finch is mistakenly believed by many of the men in town to be a talent scout for *The Manhattan Showtime* TV program. Barney plays for Finch during a shoe fitting that he thinks is really an audition. In "Mayberry on Record," Mr. Maxwell is particularly pleased with the music he has just recorded played by Andy and an unnamed band. Barney nonchalantly produces his harmonica and says, "Say, Mr. Maxwell, anytime you're ready for a little 'Que Sera Sera,' just speak up." Maxwell politely says he would, clearly having no intention of recording it. In "The Guitar Player Returns," after Bobby Fleet has rehired Jim Lindsey for his band, Jim and Andy are having an impromptu jam session with their guitars in the courthouse. Barney pulls out his harmonica from his pocket and asks, "Say, why don't I join you in the next number, huh? What'll it be?" Barney suggests "I'm Just a Vagabond Lover," "Roll Out the Barrel," "Mairzy Doats," or "Tiptoe Through the Tulips."

Without speaking, Andy takes Barney's harmonica and lays it on the desk. He and Jim then pick Barney off the floor by his bent elbows, carry him to a cell, put him inside and close the door, then come back and play another number.

Barney does not play as often during the second season but does offer to play for the beautiful Melissa Stevens and her father to impress her in "Barney on the Rebound," not realizing they are actually a husband and wife con artists. When Barney brings out his harmonica, Melissa (who is later revealed to actually be named Gladys), pretends to be impressed he has a knowledge of music. Barney explains, "I ain't ashamed to say that us rugged lawmen have our gentler moments. You know, it kinda' eases the tension after dealing with violence all day." He offers to play "Kitten on the Keys," "Roses of Picardy," and "Funiculi, Funicula." He ends up playing the public domain song "Jingle Bells." Two episodes later, after Andy plays guitar and sings "John Henry" to Otis to make him feel better, Otis asks Barney to play a song on his harmonica. Barney complains, "What is this? A jail or a nightclub?"

Near the end of the second season, Barney reveals another instrument he clearly believes he has mastered. That instrument is the conga drum though Barney mistakenly refers to it as a bongo drum. (A conga drum is a narrow Cuban drum while bongos are a pair of small joined drums of different sizes.) In "Three's a Crowd," Barney plays the drum as Thelma Lou, Andy, and Mary Simpson sing "Seeing Nellie Home" at Mary's house. As the song ends, Barney continues playing the drum by himself then finishes by yelling, "Yeah!" He then asks rhetorically, "Pretty good, huh?" When Mary politely says she thinks the drum was a nice touch, Barney excitedly asks if she would like to hear "La Cucaracha" and plays it, tossing his head at the end of each line of the song.

In the third season episode "The Mayberry Band," Barney plays a third instrument. Since he wants to join the town band, he invests in a pair of brass cymbals with leather handles. He ordered them from Cymbal City in Chicago and, going for the best, spent $18.50, four dollars more than the ones with leatherette handles. Barney says he cannot return them as he has "played" about 15 songs on them before showing them to Andy. He joins the band as standby cymbalist where he marches in place, even when rehearsing inside. Barney has been hanging around Phil Sunkel, the trumpet player for Freddy Fleet and His Band With a Beat, who had stopped in town. This is the same band that appeared in the first season although the leader earlier went by the less-alliterative name of Bobby Fleet. (The writers later admitted that the name change was because they simply forgot what the character's name was in his earlier appearances.) Sunkel's beatnik lingo rubbed off on the deputy. After Barney clashes his cymbals during rehearsal to get the town band's attention so Andy can speak, Barney says, "All right, let's cool it. Let's let Andy make the scene." He then looks at Andy and says, "Okay, gas it up, chickie."

Barney does play the harmonica one final time. In "The Loaded Goat," after Andy and Barney discover Jimmy the goat has eaten dynamite and the goat then comes into the courthouse, they first jump onto Andy's desk. Afraid Jimmy will literally explode if he butts anything and desperate to keep the goat calm, Andy asks if Barney has his French harp (another name for a harmonica) with him. Barney's playing calms the goat enough for Andy to slip a rope over the potentially-explosive animal's neck. Andy then leads Jimmy out of town while Barney walks along and plays. Andy tells him, "Play extra good. You may go down in history as the first man to ever lead a loaded goat out of town."

When was Thelma Lou first seen?

Barney's first love interest was Miss Rosemary whom he was incredibly shy to be around. Three episodes later, Hilda Mae was introduced with Barney's trademarked overconfidence on full display. After Hilda Mae was seen again for the last time in the twentieth episode, two episodes later she was replaced by the deputy's new love interest, Thelma Lou.

Betty Lynn first appears as Thelma Lou in "Cyrano Andy," broadcast on January 22, 1961. Barney has returned to being shy and is unable to tell Thelma Lou how he feels, but after a misguided attempt by Thelma Lou to make Barney jealous by pretending Andy is interested in her, the situation is finally resolved. Thelma Lou remains Barney's on-screen love interest for the rest of the black and white episodes.

Thelma Lou only appears one more time in the first season with approximately two months having passed since her first appearance. Lynn was never under a long-term contract with *The Andy Griffith Show*, instead just being used when her schedule allowed. When she first appeared as Thelma Lou, Lynn was actually under contract with The Walt Disney Company and was co-starring in their series *Texas John Slaughter* which aired between 1958 and 1961 as part of the series *Walt Disney Presents*.

Lynn appeared in half a dozen of the 31 episodes that made up the second season. She was in only five episodes of the third season, and six each in the fourth and fifth seasons, all of which consisted of 32 episodes. The net result is she appeared in only 25 episodes of the 138 episodes between her first appearance and the end of the fifth season when she left the show. Yet during the black and white years, thanks to her wonderful performance and references to her even when she was not actually on the program, Betty Lynn was as much a part of the Mayberry family as any other actor.

Lynn was asked to stay on the show when Don Knotts left but chose not to, though she did later appear as a guest star in a single color episode and was in the 1986 made-for-television reunion movie *Return to Mayberry*.

Thelma Lou is the only character seen semi-regularly who was never given a last name. Her occupation is also never clear, though a vague reference is made in the episode "Man in the Middle." When Thelma Lou and Helen are having a disagreement thanks to Barney, the deputy invites the two women to the courthouse at the same time. He asks Thelma Lou how everything is at the office and she later says she needs to get back to the office. This is the only reference made to Thelma Lou's occupation during the black and white years of *The Andy Griffith Show*.

Thelma Lou had to be very understanding while dating as dedicated a lawman as Barney Fife. After Andy offers to give

Barney the rest of the afternoon off after the deputy "caught" escaped criminal Eddie Brooke, Barney refuses, explaining to Thelma Lou, "Well, you just never know when another beast might come out of the forest. You understand, don't you, Thelma Lou?… I really don't expect you to. You see, Thelma Lou, this is what we call the deadly game. I'm in it for keeps."

In "Barney's Replacement," which is only Thelma Lou's third appearance, Barney confides to Andy that he believes he and Thelma Lou will be getting married soon. Later in the season, Thelma Lou also tells Andy that Barney is the man she wants to marry someday. When Barney once thought Thelma Lou was choosing Edgar Coleman over him, Barney assumes he and Thelma Lou are finished. He says she is the sweetest girl in the world but gone is the dream which included an ivy-covered cottage and the patter of little feet.

Unfortunately, Barney often takes Thelma Lou for granted. For example, when Gomer offers to drive Thelma Lou to Mount Pilot for a dentist's appointment, Andy teasingly asks if Barney wants to accompany them as he could lose her to a handsome man like Gomer. Barney tells Gomer he isn't worried as has Thelma Lou in his hip pocket. And, of course, Barney sees Juanita the waitress on the side while he is supposed to be keeping steady company with Thelma Lou.

After Knotts and Lynn left the series at the end of the fifth season, they both returned as guest stars the next season in "The Return of Barney Fife." In the episode, a class reunion is being held. The episode reveals that Thelma Lou moved to Jacksonville about a month after Barney left Mayberry. When Barney sees Thelma Lou at the reunion, they both admit they have often thought of one another. After they dance and she excuses herself to get her name badge, Barney tells Andy he can tell Thelma Lou is still crazy about him. In a moment antithetical to the theme of the series, when Thelma Lou returns, she is accompanied by a man she introduces as her husband, Gerald Whitfield. In her only guest appearance after leaving the series, Lynn's character finally has a last name. They have only been married six weeks at the time. Barney's cavalier attitude toward Thelma Lou certainly warrants the storyline. But the image of Mayberry as a perfect small town is shattered for at least this episode as Barney later tearfully tells Andy, "She was the only girl I ever loved, Ange. She's the only one I ever will love. I had plans. I had big plans."

"Andy Taylor, Barney Fife, I'd like you to meet my husband, Gerald Whitfield."

More than 20 years later, the situation was finally rectified when the divorced Thelma Lou and the still-single Barney were finally married in the TV movie *Return to Mayberry*.

When was Juanita first referenced and when did Andy first sneak up on Barney as the deputy was speaking to Juanita on the telephone?

There are many characters referenced in *The Andy Griffith Show* who are never actually seen. One of the best known is Juanita, the waitress at the diner. As Barney's character evolved, by the end of the first season he is playing the field in spite of having a steady girlfriend, Thelma Lou.

Juanita is first mentioned in episode 28 of the first season, "Andy Forecloses," originally aired on April 24, 1961. When Barney does not want to let Andy look at his filled citation book, it is because he has more than citations written in it. Andy discovers the name Juanita Beasley and her telephone number in the book and recognizes the name. She is a new waitress at the Junction Cafe, a restaurant presumably

at a major intersection on the edge of town since truck drivers stop there to eat. Barney explains why he has her work telephone number by saying he calls there occasionally for "trouble checks" to be sure everything is okay. At the end of the episode, after Andy and Ben Weaver leave to go fishing and Barney stays behind, Andy waits a moment then quietly opens the door to find Barney sweet talking Juanita over the phone before singing the song "Juanita" to her. Andy loudly joins in on the refrain, startling, frustrating, and then angering Barney.

By the second season, Juanita works at the diner, which is eventually named as the Bluebird Diner in the third season.

The romantic song Barney begins to sing in "Andy Forecloses" is also sometimes called "Nita Juanita." Written in 1853, it was the first ballad written by a female composer to attain massive sales of its sheet music. A few years earlier in the 1950s series *Father Knows Best*, Jim Anderson serenaded his wife with the song while playing the banjo. Bing Crosby had included it as part of a medley on an album released early in 1961. "Andy Forecloses" was broadcast in April 1961 and was obviously filmed weeks earlier. It is possible the use of this public domain song's lyrics was what led to the character being named Juanita in the first place.

It was a good thing Andy interrupted Barney before the second refrain. The full lyrics of the refrains are:

> Nita! Juanita! Ask thy soul if we should part!
> Nita! Juanita! Lean thou on my heart.
>
> Nita! Juanita! Let me linger by thy side!
> Nita! Juanita! Be my own fair bride!

When was Helen Crump first seen?

After the planned courtship of Ellie Walker by Andy and eventual marriage between the two did not work out, the show's producers introduced several different love interests for the sheriff though none were long term. Andy Griffith later said they just didn't know how to write for women on the show and he was never comfortable playing love scenes.

Aneta Corsaut was dating Jim Fritzell, a regular writer on *The Andy Griffith Show*. Fritzell put in a good word for her with story consultant Aaron Ruben and regular director Bob Sweeney which led to Corsaut being cast in a role that was intended to be a one-shot, that of Opie's new teacher, Helen Crump, in "Andy Discovers America" which premiered near the end of the third season on March 4, 1963. In the episode, Andy is stunned to see the beautiful Helen after Opie and his friends described her as "old lady Crump."

The spark that had been missing from past attempts was finally found in the introduction of a character who did not hesitate to stand up to Andy. This was in part a reflection of the actors' actual relationship. When Corsaut and Griffith first met on set, they got into a heated argument about something related to feminism and were soon yelling at one another. Griffith was impressed by the sharp-tongued Corsaut who felt free to disagree with him. Recalling Andy, Corsaut said, "There were obsequious people who came on the show who would try to butter him up, and he didn't like that. I think he respected the fact that I stood up for what I believed."

A few episodes later on April 15, 1963, Helen appears for the second time in "A Wife for Andy." After Barney at first thinks Helen might be the future Mrs. Andy Taylor, he decides she is not right for Andy when he discovers she cannot cook and does not plan to quit her job when she marries. At the end of the episode, Andy tells Barney he has decided he is going to court Helen.

Oddly enough, when Helen is next seen in the eighth episode of the following season, while friendly, Andy greets the woman he is supposed to be courting by saying, "Well, hey, Miss Crump." She responds, "Hello, Sheriff." But afterward, they are clearly dating. Of course, even odder is the fact that Helen continually moves up a grade in teaching so that Opie is always in her class.

During the fourth season, Helen appears at roughly the same rate as Thelma Lou, with five appearances. But in the remaining seasons, she becomes more of a mainstay character though she never appears in a majority of the episodes in any of the seasons. Andy and Helen finally marry on the first episode of *Mayberry R.F.D.* with Barney serving as best man.

The last name "Crump" may have been inspired by a town called Crumpler which is less than 60 miles west of Andy Griffith's hometown of Mount Airy, North Carolina.

When was Sarah the telephone operator first referenced?

Just like the waitress Juanita, telephone operator Sarah is a fan-favorite character even though she is never actually seen or heard on the show though she is certainly spoken to.

Andy and Opie are the only two characters seen in the pilot who are also seen in the series, but the character of Sarah is also referenced in "Danny Meets Andy Griffith" and continues to be referenced many times in the spin-off.

In the February 15, 1960 pilot episode, an incensed Danny Williams demands to make a phone call, telling Andy he is going to call the local paper to expose the sheriff as corrupt. When Danny picks up the phone, he asks, "Hello, operator?" Andy helpfully tells him, "Name's Sarah."

While Mayberry residents are the ones usually shown talking to Sarah, just as in the pilot, it is a non-resident who first speaks to her in the series. In the second episode, "Manhunt," first seen October 19, 1960, Captain Barker and a regiment of the State Police roll into town to set up a manhunt for an escaped convict. As Andy follows them into the courthouse, Captain Barker is on the phone telling the operator he want the line kept open to the state capital. Sarah presumably responds, "Who says so?" as Barker momentarily looks at the phone with surprise, then says, "Captain Barker, State Police. That's who says so." Andy then takes the phone and calls Sarah by her name.

Presumably, Sarah runs the switchboard in a room of her house. When Andy is at Sam Becker's late at night and has to call Aunt Bee, he apologizes to Sarah for waking her.

When placing a call, people sometimes have to chat with Sarah a bit before the call is placed. The amount of chatting increases as the series continues. Initially, when Captain Barker tells Sarah to keep a line open to the capital, Andy takes the phone and explains, "It's all right. Any sheriff business comes up, why, you can call my home phone. All right." Then in response to an unheard question asked by Sarah undoubtedly about Aunt Bee, Andy answers, "Oh, she's fine."

This type of exchange obviously results in the audience hearing only one side of the conversation. Eventually, the exchanges grow in length for additional comedic effect. For example, while Andy is trying to place a call, the viewers hear Andy responding to Sarah, "Oh, oh, that's a shame. Well, drink a lot of hot juices." Other examples include, "Fine. How are you? (pause) Well, you got to gargle a lot, Sarah," and "Soak it, Sarah. Soak it a lot in warm salt water."

Sarah is not above gossiping about telephone calls on which she eavesdrops, once telling Aunt Bee (who later explains to Andy she wasn't gossiping herself, just listening) about the new barber at Floyd's being popular with the ladies. Both Sarah and Aunt Bee do not realize the "barber" is, in fact, a bookie taking bets. Aunt Bee thinks from the names and habits conveyed by Sarah, the ladies might be chorus girls. For example, Tiger Lil didn't come home until 10 to 1!

Sarah is also not shy about offering advice after eavesdropping. Concerned about not having forwarded a chain letter, Barney takes Andy's advice and decides to call Thelma Lou to arrange a date for the evening. Sarah apparently asks where Thelma Lou is. Barney responds, "How should I know? You're the phone operator." When

Thelma Lou tells him she was not available, Barney angrily asks, "Well, which is more important? Me or gluing covers back on hymn books with Edgar Coleman?" (Edgar is another of the many characters referenced who were never seen, helping to give the show the feeling of being a real town.) After Barney angrily tells Thelma Lou she needs to choose between him and Edgar Coleman and speaks out of turn, Thelma Lou hangs up on him. When Andy suggests Barney call her back, the deputy instead picks up the receiver and says, "Sarah, get me Juanita down at the diner." Sarah obviously feels free to offer her opinion as Barney then blurts, "I don't care whether you think I ought to call Juanita or not! Just get her!" Barney then looks at Andy, points at the phone, and complains Sarah was "[l]istenin' in again!"

Throughout the series, the audience learns various facts about Sarah, such as she enjoys a pinch of snuff every now and then and that her mother once hurt her hip from a fall at the bowling alley. Such one-sided dialogue made Sarah seem as real as any of the Mayberry residents.

Griffith was well known for using names of relatives and people he knew as character names in *The Andy Griffith Show*. As previously mentioned, he likely chose the name "Taylor" because it was the maiden name of his paternal grandmother. And that same paternal grandmother's first name? Sarah.

When was Barney first shown to be overconfident in his memorization skills?

While not a gag used often in the series, two scenes of Barney being shown to have poor memorization skills yet still feel supremely confident in his abilities are among fans' favorites.

The first time this is seen was in the fourth episode, "Ellie Comes to Town," aired on October 24, 1960. After being in the drugstore while Emma Brand tries to sneak in to get her pills without a prescription, Andy returns to the courthouse to find Barney studying a book to memorize the "Sheriff's Rules." Barney tells him he has the first one memorized, which oddly was located approximately a third of the way through a fairly thick book instead of near the beginning. Regardless, Barney hands Andy the book and asks him to check his memorization, assuring him he knows the whole thing.

When Andy tells him to go ahead, Barney furrows his brow and after a long pause, asks for the first word. When Andy tells him it is "An," Barney repeats the word twice then a third time as a question. After Barney asks "An?" and Andy affirms it is the first word, Barney looks confused and asks if Andy is sure. Andy responds, "I'm lookin' right at it." After another moment, Barney asks for the second word. Andy tells him "officer" and Barney responds, "Oh, yeah, 'An officer.' 'An officer...'" and can get no further, eventually putting his head in his hands while leaning on his table and repeating "An officer" more than half a dozen times trying to remember the next word.

Andy finally tells him, "An officer of the" and Barney repeats it. Andy then asks, "An officer of the what?" and Barney responds declaratively, "An officer of the what!" He then stops and says that doesn't sound right. Andy says it isn't and that the rule begins "An officer of the law." Andy then has to feed Barney the rest of the rule word by word which Barney repeats until he is done. Andy then asks Barney if he wants to go over it again or if he thinks he has it. With his arms crossed, the self-satisfied Barney says, "I got it."

Early in the fourth season, the Sheriff's Rules gag is expanded although this rendition involves the Preamble to the Constitution. In a favorite scene of many fans of *The Andy Griffith Show*, in "Opie's Ill-Gotten Gain," Barney brings his eighth-grade history book into the courthouse. Barney tells Andy there are things in the book he still remembers, adding, "It's amazin' how that stuff stays with you. Once you learn somethin', it never leaves you. Just stays locked up tight in the ole' noodle." He decides to show Andy this is true by pointing out he had to memorize the Preamble in eighth grade and still remembers it. Just like in the gag from the first season, Barney hands Andy the book then cannot remember the first word. When Andy says it is "We," Barney asks it as a question, "We?" just as he had in the first season. And again, just as in the original gag, Barney looks confused and asks if Andy is sure, prompting Andy to again answer, "I'm lookin' right at it."

Barney is told the second word is "the" and then needs help with the third. Andy purses his lips to show the sound of the first letter as a clue for the word "people" and Barney also purses his lips trying to get the word. Once he knows the first three words are, "We the people," just as he had during the first season, Barney puts his head in his hands

while leaning on his table trying to summon the next word. After being fed enough individual words to get to "We the people of the United," Barney cannot come up with "States" as the next word. Andy tries to give him a clue by holding onto the American flag behind his desk. Barney then guesses, "Flag?" After Andy shakes his head no and then moves the fabric of the flag, Barney guesses, "Breeze? Wind? Wave?" Andy then points to the stars on the flag and Barney yells, "Stars!" Andy immediately corrects him, "States!" which Barney then repeats triumphantly as if he had figured it out.

Andy feeds him the next partial phrase "in order to form a more perfect" a word or two at a time, then says only the "u" sound at the beginning of the next word, "union." Barney then says, "To form a more perfect you." As Andy continues to feed Barney the words, he gives Barney only syllables when he gets to the word "establish." Barney repeats, "Es. Ta. Bli." When Andy voices the "Sh" sound, Barney takes it as a shushing sound, puts the sounds together, and whispers, "Establi." When Andy gives him only part of the next word "justice," Barney thinks it is the entire word, saying, "Establish just."

Andy goes through the rest of the Preamble with Barney not even repeating many of the words but nodding along until the conclusion. Just as he had in the earlier Sheriff's Rules version of the gag, Andy asks Barney if he wants to go over it again or if he thinks he has it. With his arms crossed, the self-satisfied Barney says, "I got it. When you learn somethin', you learn it."

In both of these scenes, but especially in the first season version with the Sheriff's Rules, Griffith clearly is having a difficult time getting through the scene without laughing. In the first season version, as Griffith is feeding him the rule word by word, Knotts is also clearly fighting to keep a straight face.

When scripts were turned in and needed a bit of padding for the timing of the episode to work, Griffith and Knotts would often plan a small gag such as this that was not truly related to the storyline of the episode but were hilarious. They improvised these memorization gags just as they did with various other "bits" that made the show so entertaining with the gags then incorporated into the written script to allow for the camera angles to be planned. Story consultant Aaron Ruben said that the original idea to use this particular gag came from Knotts who originally pitched it as Barney needing to memorize the Sheriff's Rules to qualify for a raise. Assistant Director Bruce Bilson remembered being in the room during a script read through and saw the genesis the routine. Knotts wrote a version of the sheriff's rules himself by hand on a piece of paper then handed it to Griffith and asked him to quiz him to demonstrate how the gag would work.

The two actors enjoyed this particular exchange so much they would often perform it at parties. They also did a version of the same gag but with Barney trying to demonstrate he had memorized the Gettysburg Address during a skit in a mid-1960s television special.

The memorization gag itself was inspired by a similar scene in Mark Twain's *The Adventures of Tom Sawyer* when Tom struggles to remember Bible verses from the Sermon on the Mount which he had specifically chosen for memorization because they were short. He has to be coached in a similar fashion, as shown in this interchange between Tom and his cousin, Mary, with Tom speaking first.

> "Blessed are the—a—a—"
> "Poor"—
> "Yes—poor; blessed are the poor—a—a—"
> "In spirit—"
> "In spirit; blessed are the poor in spirit, for they—they—"
> "Theirs—"
> "For theirs. Blessed are the poor in spirit, for theirs is the kingdom of heaven. Blessed are they that mourn, for they—they—"
> "Sh—"
> "For they—a—"
> "S, H, A—"
> "For they S, H—Oh, I don't know what it is!"
> "Shall!"
> "Oh, shall!

Barney did once offer a way to memorize dates which he believed would "revolutionize the whole world of modern education" in the third season episode, "Andy Discovers America." Using 1776 as an example, Barney says the first number is easy to remember because one is "the first number in the alphabet." For the second number, he says to just remember "lucky seven" and the third number is "easy to remember 'cause you just remembered seven, see?" To get the fourth number, all one needs to do is just remember "[w]hat's one from seven?" When Andy asks if it wouldn't be easier just to remember 1776, Barney says, "Well, if you want to do things the easy way you're never gonna' learn anything."

When was the first time Barney's hair was shown to be disheveled?

Seeing Barney's hair in disarray became a recurring gag in *The Andy Griffith Show*. In the first season alone, it is seen multiple times. Sometimes it is the result of exertion by the thin but wiry deputy, such as when trying to demonstrate the art of judo. Sometimes it is the result of others, such as Hilda Mae running her fingers through his hair. Sometimes it is even done by Barney himself out of irritation, such as when Andy sneaks up on Barney during a telephone conversation with Juanita. But the first time was in the fourth episode, "Ellie Comes to Town," first aired October 24, 1960, during the previously discussed demonstration of his memorization of the "Sheriff's Rules."

At the point in the scene when Andy had tells Barney the first words are "An officer of the law," Barney repeats the words with his hands locked behind his head. As he strains to remember the next word, Barney turns and leans his elbows on his table. He runs his fingers through his hair and as he turns back toward Andy, his hair is comically out of place.

The visual gag is repeated over three years later in Season 4 using the Preamble to the Constitution which Barney insists he still remembers from eighth grade. At the point where Barney only has been fed the words "We the people," he again turns and leans on his table with his head in his hands. In the Preamble version of the gag, as Barney turns back toward Andy, his hair has not only been pulled down into his face but the corners of his lips are pulled comically downward.

However, just before Andy grabs the American flag

to give Barney a hint, the deputy's hair is now back in place and neatly combed. As the scene progresses, whenever the camera shot is on Barney alone, his hair is disheveled. But in all the shots in which both Andy and Barney are in the frame together, Barney's hair is in place.

The Andy Griffith Show was shot with a single camera, just as a film would have been. As a result, scenes would have to be repeated and filmed more than once to capture different angles. This resulted in this blooper with Barney's hair alternating from being disheveled to being in place.

After Hilda Mae ran her fingers through Barney's hair in "Andy Saves Barney's Morale."

When did Barney first use the phrase "Nip it?"

Over the course of the show, Barney's use of the phrase "Nip it!" or some variation became a classic catchphrase. Barney actually does not say the phrase until nearly midway through the second season. He first says it in the January 1, 1962 episode "The Farmer Takes a Wife." He speaks the phrase to Thelma Lou when she is being courted by farmer Jeff Pruitt, firmly telling her she needs to "Nip it! Nip it in the bud!" It is not hard to see why the writers would want to make this a catchphrase of Barney's, as Don Knotts' delivery of the line so emphatically is hilarious from the beginning.

Barney goes on to use the phrase or some variation of it many times, including eight episodes later when he has obviously instructed his three temporary deputies as to what they are to do the minute they think there might be trouble at Founder's Day. He then asks the deputies, "You got that? Let's hear it!" to which they all shout in unison, "Nip it!" with Floyd adding, "in the bud!" Howard McNear's delivery of the line is also laugh-out-loud funny.

Another example of Barney's use of the phrase is found in the episode "One-Punch Opie." Concerned a new boy in town is leading local youngsters astray, Barney warns Andy, "Today's eight-year-olds are tomorrow's teenagers. I say this calls for action and now! Nip it in the bud! First sign a youngster's goin' wrong, you got to nip it in the bud." After Andy says he is going to have a talk with the boys, Barney adds, "Nip it. You go read any book you want on the subject of child discipline, and you'll find that every one of 'em is in favor of bud nippin.'"

The phrase is not a new one. It derived from the de-budding of plants and came to be a phrase meaning to put a stop to something while still early in development. The phrase's earlier form from the 16th century was "nip in the bloom." Barney's use of such an old-fashioned phrase made it all the funnier. Writer Harvey Bullock noted *The Andy Griffith Show* "just gave you free rein to go back into those stuffy old-maid, old school-time words you'd used."

It is lost to history exactly how the phrase was given to Barney. Writer Everett Greenbaum believed he came up with the idea. While on his honeymoon, Greenbaum was driving down a steep hill in low gear causing a loud whining sound in the car. He said his new wife knew so little about machinery "she thought that if you flushed the toilet too many times, the electric bill would go up." At the bottom of the hill when Greenbaum was able to shift back to a higher gear and the whining stopped, his newlywed wife told him, "Well, you nipped that in the bud." Recalling this when he began writing scripts for *The Andy Griffith Show*, he said he started using it.

However, as mentioned, the first time Barney said the phrase in the series was in the episode "The Farmer Takes a Wife" which first aired on New Year's Day of 1962 well before Greenbaum ever used it in a script. "The Farmer Takes a Wife" was written by Charles Stewart and Jack Elinson.

Stewart and Elinson also wrote the episode mentioned above with the three Founder's Day deputies, "Guest of Honor" which aired on February 26, 1962. But the writing duo's use of the phrase to nip something in the bud actually pre-dated *The Andy Griffith Show* itself. Stewart and Elinson were frequent writers for the series *The Real McCoys*. On April 10, 1958, an episode they wrote titled "Kate's Career" aired which shows Luke McCoy first using the phrase in reference to stopping his wife from pursuing a dress alteration business. (The character uses the phrase again in later episodes.) Luke was played by Richard Crenna whose delivery of the phrase did not have the same distinctiveness as when delivered by Don Knotts as the excitable Barney Fife.

Certainly, the expression is an old one used by many. Two and a half years after Stewart and Elinson first used the phrase in an episode of *The Real McCoys*, Greenbaum and Fritzel did as well in an episode they wrote for *McCoys* though it was a guest star who used the phrase instead of one of the McCoys. So Greenbaum had actually used the phrase in a script of *The Real McCoys* years before he used it in the Mayberry series.

Regardless, while "Nip it in the bud!" first appeared in *The Andy Griffith Show* in Stewart and Elinson's "The Farmer Takes a Wife," the catchphrase became one used by several writers on *The Andy Griffith Show* as it quickly became a running gag, one which Don Knotts said he liked playing.

"And it's got to stop right now. Nip it! Nip it in the bud!"

When was barber Floyd Lawson first seen?

The character of Floyd the town barber is introduced in the twelfth episode of the inaugural season, "Stranger in Town," which first aired on December 26, 1960. The character's name was inspired by Floyd Pike, a successful businessman Andy knew in Mount Airy, who also lent his last name to Mayor Pike.

In his first appearance, Floyd was played by Walter Baldwin. The barber's last name is not given in the episode. The married, clean-shaven character is older than the Floyd most fans know and love. This Floyd has r h e u m a t i s m and is prone to napping in the barber chair between customers.

Floyd as played by Walter Baldwin.

He wears glasses and even when wearing them cannot see well from a distance. Baldwin was nearly 72 years old when the episode was aired.

Baldwin was quite nervous and had trouble remembering his lines, so the series producers quickly decided to go with a younger actor. Thus, Baldwin only played Floyd once. He was replaced by the 55-year-old Howard McNear in literally the next episode to air, "Mayberry Goes Hollywood," first broadcast on January 2, 1961. McNear's

Floyd has a mustache and, while he still wears glasses, his poor eyesight is not an issue. He is a member of the town council and like most other residents, "went Hollywood" when a movie was to be filmed in town. Floyd's last name was still not spoken at that point, but according to new signage in the window in anticipation of

Floyd as played by Howard McNear.

the arrival of a Hollywood film crew, it was Colby.

In McNear's third appearance in the episode "The Beauty Contest" which first aired January 23, 1961, Floyd composed a song to be sung after the crowning of Miss Mayberry, the title given to the winner of the Founder's Day beauty pageant. A writer in the *Mayberry Gazette* mentions that fact in an article about the song, calling him Floyd Lawson, the first time the name he is known by the rest of the series is used.

The popularity of Floyd is due in large part to the brilliance of McNear. Cast members uniformly said he was similar to the character he was playing. His line delivery made it difficult for his fellow cast members to keep straight faces. In the first seasons, McNear's frenetic, nervous mannerisms and hesitant speaking style supply some of the series' funniest moments. Aaron Ruben recalled that even during the table read throughs held before actual filming occurred "Andy [Griffith] would slide on the floor when Howard opened his mouth. Not reading the script... just talking about something that happened that morning."

Before Floyd was introduced, the window of the barbershop said the barber's name was Sid Elson, but in McNear's first appearance as Floyd, Andy tells Mr. Harmon who wants to make a film in Mayberry that Floyd has "been barbering folks around here since most of us was just young 'uns" and Floyd indicates he is the only barber in town.

During the first season, Floyd's unseen wife is named Melba. One of Floyd's children is seen in "Those Gossipin' Men," Floyd's second appearance. The dialogue is not clear, but according to the script, the son's name is Windell. In the second season episode "The Jinx," another son named Norman is mentioned. However, by this point, Floyd is a widower.

Floyd is featured as the central character of an episode only once. In the third season's "Floyd, the Gay Deceiver," the widowed Floyd has joined a Lonely Hearts Correspondence Club and posed as a wealthy businessman in order to measure up to who he believes is a wealthy widow. He tells Andy it is only natural as he is a lonely widower. Floyd is at his most animated after having confessed what he has done to Andy, repeatedly looking at his own reflection and calling himself a "miserable wretch" and repeatedly saying he is going to leave town for Nashville so his correspondent will not have to learn the truth about him. Andy and Aunt Bee help Floyd pose as a wealthy man but Andy then learns the woman Floyd has been writing is actually a scam artist. He refrains from telling Floyd to spare his feelings.

"Floyd, the Gay Deceiver" is one of only seven episodes written by *The Andy Griffith Show*'s story consultant and driving force Aaron Ruben. While he knew McNear was a modest man, Ruben did not at first realize McNear would be so nervous about serving as the central character. Ruben recalled, "[H]e was absolutely terrified about doing that show. Shortly before we were to shoot, he called me up and he said, 'Oh, oh, oh, I don't think you should…uhm, uh, make me the ah, ah, star of that story. I—I…' He was scared silly. I said, 'Now, Howard, it's gonna' work. It's gonna' be great, you'll see.'"

While "Floyd, the Gay Deceiver" was centered on Floyd, he is also featured heavily two episodes later in "Convicts-at-Large," an episode which involves Barney and Floyd being held captive in a secluded cabin by three escaped female convicts. Floyd quickly becomes somewhat acclimated to the captivity and is soon referring to Barney as "Al" just as escaped convict Sally does since Barney reminds her of a former flame thanks to Barney, like Al, having "[t]hat same dumb face…the weak chin…and round shoulders."

Howard McNear suffered a stroke shortly after filming "Convicts-at-Large" which originally aired December 10, 1962. The show quickly felt the loss of such a wonderful comedic actor who was seen so frequently in Mayberry.

"Yeah, gee whiz. Two chairs…and I got the magazines to swing it!"

When was Mayor Stoner first seen?

Mayor Pike was played by Dick Elliott who passed away in December 1961, midway through the second season. While the character of a mayor was not integral to the series, Mayor Pike was a comical and loved character.

In the third season, the decision was made to add a new mayor. However, Mayor Roy Stoner is not an inherently humorous character. Rather, he is an irksome, officious character who is a constant irritant to Andy.

Mayor Stoner first appears in "Andy and the New Mayor," originally broadcast October 15, 1963. When discussing a scheduled meeting, Andy mentions to Barney the new mayor will be on time as he has just been elected. Stoner is irritated with Andy from the beginning, angry that Andy is late for their first meeting. When Andy walks into the mayor's office and says good morning, Stoner does not reply and instead takes out his pocket watch and stares at it. When Andy says he is sorry he is late, Stoner snidely asks, "Well, we won't make a habit of it, will we?" When Andy sees empty chairs and says he thought there was a meeting, Stoner replies there was "an hour and six minutes ago," then clicks his pocket watch shut.

Andy Griffith did not like the concept of Mayor Stoner being added to the series. He said, "[T]he only fight Sheldon [Leonard] and I ever had in my whole acquaintanceship with him was over a story idea. He wanted to introduce a character that I knew wasn't gonna' work. And it didn't. It was the mayor. They wanted me to have a boss figure." Griffith acknowledged it was not a bad idea for a lead character to have a boss but argued it would not make sense in the series.

"I told them before we started, that can't work because the mayor cannot be a boss to the sheriff. The sheriff's a county official. A mayor's just a little local town official. So it didn't work. He stayed on for one season and just did infrequent appearances. But, that's the only fight Sheldon and I ever had."

As Griffith pointed out, a mayor would legally have no power over a county sheriff. The writers tried to get around this fact by having Stoner say he had connections at the state level and could make things difficult for Andy. For example, when Andy defends himself for not carrying a gun, Stoner tells him he plans to send a report on every department to the governor's office. When Stoner later learns Andy has allowed a prisoner to leave the cell to get his crops in with the promise he would return to finish his sentence, Stoner angrily tells Andy, "Sheriff, you'd better go out there and find him and bring him back!" When Andy said the farmer will be there, Stoner says, "Sheriff, you'd better see to it because after the governor hears about this, somebody else might just be wearing that badge!" tapping Andy's badge with the cell keys he is holding.

Stoner is understandably not a popular character with fans of The Andy Griffith Show, but in fairness, he was not meant to be. He was meant to be exactly as irritating as the skilled actor Parley Baer played him.

Of course, the mayor inevitably gets his comeuppance at the end of episodes. When the farmer who has been temporarily released to gather his crops does not return on time, Stoner insists they go to his house to try to locate him. They find him in a tree refusing to come down. Stoner rushes to the tree to try to bring him down only to discover the man is in the tree because he is seeking refuge from a bear. Scratched and with torn clothes, Stoner scampers up the tree himself. The same general pattern repeats through all of Stoner's appearances. When the mayor is convinced Andy cannot solve the thefts of cows in the area, he calls in the investigator William Upchurch of the Special Investigation section. By the end of the episode, it is Andy's common sense that solves the crime. When the mayor does not want to approve the Mayberry Band's trip to the capital, Andy is able to use the visiting musicians of Freddy Fleet and His Band with a Beat to trick the mayor and finally get the funding.

While the mayor's stated connections to the governor were previously used to threaten Andy, when Barney tickets the governor's car in "Barney and the Governor," it becomes clear Stoner's connections are not as he implied. After Andy refuses to call the governor to apologize for Barney issuing the citation, Stoner calls the governor himself from the courthouse. While waiting for the governor to pick up, he tells Andy, "I just want him to know that we're not all stupid down here. The best thing for me is to talk to the governor himself. Fortunately, I know him. It may make things a little easier." When he is put through to the governor, Stoner calls him by his first name but the governor does not know who he is. In an at-first gushing voice, Stoner says, "Hello, Ed. How are ya'? Long time, no see. Look, Ed... Uh, Stoner. Roy Stoner? Look, Ed, your car was passing through... Stoner. S-T-O-N-E-R. Stoner." The mayor gets an immediate comeuppance when he gives the phone to Andy and the governor tells the sheriff he views what Barney has done as commendable. The governor adds he wants to come to Mayberry to shake Barney's hand. By the end of the episode, Stoner becomes accidentally intoxicated and misses the governor's visit altogether while sleeping it off.

The mayor is not above using his political position to help his own family. In "The Loaded Goat," the dynamite being stored in town is being used for blasting in the construction of a new underpass. The mayor's real purpose in doing so is to bring the highway past his brother's filling station.

Stoner's last appearance is in "Rafe Hollister Sings," the 20th episode of the third season. With still a dozen episodes to go, Stoner actually lasted less than three-quarters of the season. In the episode, Mayor Stoner sides with the snooty Mrs. Jeffries, head of the local chapter of the Ladies League. When the rough-around-the-edges Rafe is selected to represent the town and sing at the musicale, Stoner and Jeffries object. After they see Rafe in a suit which Andy has tricked him into wearing, they reluctantly agree it will be acceptable so long as Rafe does not associate with anyone. The haughty couple are put in their place when Andy has Rafe appear on stage wearing his normal bib overalls and the musicale organizer is thrilled with his moving performance.

When was Gomer Pyle first seen?

The character of Floyd Lawson had become an important secondary comic character who appeared periodically in *The Andy Griffith Show*. When Howard McNear suffered a stroke and was forced to leave the show, the need for another comic character became all the more urgent.

Gomer Pyle is first introduced in "The Bank Job," just two episodes after McNear's final episode before the stroke. In "The Bank Job," which aired Christmas Eve, 1962, an undercover Barney wearing woman's clothes is accidentally locked in the vault at the Mayberry Security Bank. Gomer is summoned from the filling station to try to cut through the safe door with an acetylene torch. He is apparently competent enough to do at least some auto body work, as he explains cutting through the vault door isn't as easy as cutting through a "mashed" fender. The character is referred to by only his first name.

Three episodes later, Gomer is seen for the second time in the January 14, 1963 episode "Man in a Hurry." Andy uses the full name of Gomer Pyle when explaining to stranded businessman Malcolm Tucker that Gomer will be in charge of the filling station since it is a Sunday. When Gomer tries to diagnose the cause of Mr. Tucker's car troubles, he says, "Could be your gauge. Sometimes she'll tell you 'F' when you really got yourself a 'E.' 'E' means that it's empty. 'F' means that it's full." Andy then tells Mr. Tucker that Gomer is not a mechanic. Later in the episode, Gomer also says, "Of course, I don't fix 'em. I just put in the gas."

"Man in a Hurry" was actually filmed before "The Bank Job." Episodes were not necessarily broadcast in the order filmed.

In fact, while Gomer was introduced to the public just two episodes after McNear's stroke, three weeks actually elapsed between the filming of McNear's last episode and Nabor's first.

By early in the next season, Gomer is now an excellent mechanic who can diagnose problems with a car just from the sound alone, as seen in "Gomer, the House Guest." The show's producers were not worried the audience would be bothered by the change in the character. They were more concerned about telling a good story than strict consistency.

Andy Griffith had already figured out they would likely lose Jim Nabors to another network if they did not lock him into a new television vehicle. Griffith said as much to Aaron Ruben and insisted Ruben develop a new series for Nabors. Well aware of the comedic possibilities of a country bumpkin thrust into the officious and regimented world of the military from Griffith's own portrayal of Will Stockdale in *No Time for Sergeants*, Ruben created *Gomer Pyle-USMC*.

It was a meteoric rise for Nabors who had never acted before being cast as Gomer. Nabors did have a comedic nightclub act where he would speak in the same voice he later used for Gomer but then sing in his rich baritone voice. Griffith saw him perform the act at a club called The Horn in Santa Monica which led to Nabors quickly being cast as Gomer.

The role was created by frequent Mayberry writers Everett Greenbaum and Jim Fritzell. The writing pair had been tasked with writing the character of Wally but were having trouble making the owner of the filling station funny enough to satisfy themselves. (By the way, that name was likely chosen as a nod to Wallace Smith who owned a Mount Airy service station that Griffith's father frequented.) Greenbaum later recalled he was driving to a story meeting and his car was not working properly. He pulled into a garage and the attendant literally said the line Gomer used when he first met Mr. Tucker in "Man in a Hurry," explaining that sometimes the gauge might show you an "F" when you really had an "E," prompting Greenbaum to propose a dimwitted gas station attendant for the scene.

The character's first name of Gomer was chosen as an homage to the writer Gomer Cool, who wrote for radio and eventually became the president of the Radio Writers Guild and then second vice-president of the Writers Guild of America West. Most sources, including the seminal book *The Andy Griffith Show* by Richard Kelly, have stated the name of Pyle was taken from well-known actor Denver Pyle who, 11 episodes after the filming of Gomer's first appearance, filmed his debut in Mayberry as Briscoe Darling, the patriarch of the Darling family. Denver Pyle was known not just as a busy actor to Greenbaum and Fritzell. He appeared in an episode of *The Real McCoys* they wrote which closed the third season of that series in 1960. Denver Pyle had also become friends with the writers and others of the Mayberry cast. However, at least one source states the last name of Pyle was instead taken from Denver's older sister, Skippy, who was Sheldon Leonard's administrative assistant whom he thought highly of and relied on heavily. Regardless, it was their family name that was used for Gomer.

As was the norm with new characters on the show, Gomer was originally introduced in *The Andy Griffith Show* as a one-shot character without a contract, but the producers quickly realized Gomer could pick up much of the comedic slack caused by McNear's stroke.

The pilot for the spin-off series *Gomer Pyle-USMC* was the twelfth episode filmed during Season 4 of *The Andy Griffith Show* and was immediately picked up by sponsor General

Foods which also sponsored the parent show. However, the pilot was not aired until months later as the final episode of the season on May 18, 1964. The episode title itself used the grammatically correct "Gomer Pyle, U.S.M.C" but the spin-off series was stylized by CBS as *Gomer Pyle-USMC*. The pilot was written by Ruben and was one of only two episodes of *The Andy Griffith Show* he directed, the other being the season opener for the fifth season, "Opie Loves Helen." Ruben had previously directed 31 episodes of *The Phil Silvers Show*, popularly known as *Sgt. Bilko*. Ruben went on to also direct "Gomer Overcomes the Obstacle Course," the first episode of the new series which premiered September 25, 1964. He later also directed the premier episode of the second season.

Gomer Pyle-USMC was a huge success, never falling out of the top ten shows in the Nielsen ratings. It ended its first season the third most-watched show in the country and reached number two the following season. While its ratings dropped its third season when it was moved by the network from its regular Friday night time slot to Wednesdays, it still managed to rank as number ten. CBS

then moved it back to Friday nights for the remaining two seasons where it rose back to number three during the fourth season and was the second most-watched show in the country its final season.

When did Gomer first say "Shazam?"

When Gomer Pyle was first introduced in "The Bank Job" which aired on Christmas Eve, 1962, he did not use his now-well-known expression of surprise. Nor did he say it during his second or third appearances. It was on February 25, 1963, during the fourth time Gomer was seen, that he first said, "Shazam!" In "The Great Filling Station Robbery," thefts are occurring overnight at Wally's Filling Station even though all the doors and windows are locked and there is no sign of forced entry. In an attempt to use modern technology to catch the criminal, Barney secures a camera aimed at the door and ties a string with one end attached to the shutter and the other attached to the door across the room so when the door is opened, the camera will take a photo of the criminal. After Barney explains the complicated apparatus, Gomer is impressed with the ingenuity. He says, "Shazam!" then adds, "Captain Marvel wouldn't have thought of that, Barney!"

Gomer was a great fan of comic books and clearly enjoyed *Captain Marvel*. However, while Gomer still read comic books as an adult, he likely would have read the Captain Marvel comics when he was younger. It had been a decade since they were published by the time the episode aired in 1963. Captain Marvel was a superhero who appeared in a line of comic books published by Fawcett Comics beginning in December 1939 (though the comic book issue in which he first appeared was dated on the cover as February 1940 in an attempt to keep it on newsstands longer, a common industry practice). In the comics, a child named Billy Batson met a wizard named Shazam who granted him the ability to transform into the adult Captain Marvel by saying the magic word, "Shazam." DC Comics, who had first published Superman in April 1938 (dated on the cover as June 1938), thought Fawcett's creation of "Earth's Mightiest Mortal" to be too similar to their own property. It did not help that *Captain Marvel* titles became the most popular comic books published in the 1940s, outselling *Superman*. DC eventually filed suit to stop Fawcett, alleging that Captain Marvel was basically a copy of their character, Superman. Partially as a result of the lawsuit, Fawcett agreed to stop publishing the comics in 1953. Thus, Gomer could not have seen any new issues in quite some time.

By the way, the magic word "Shazam" stood for superhuman powers Captain Marvel was granted: the wisdom of Solomon, the strength of Hercules, the stamina of Atlas, the power of Zeus, the courage of Achilles, and the speed of Mercury.

"Shazam" became a catchphrase for Gomer. He used it in another appearance late in Season 3 then used it often the following season. The day the gold truck came through Mayberry, Gomer not only uses the word three times in the same episode, Andy even says it himself. After Barney tells Gomer the gold has been hijacked, Gomer responds, "Shazam!" After Andy explains to Barney and Gomer that the gold truck was a decoy, Gomer says two times in a row, "A decoy! Shazam!" When Barney then repeats, "A decoy," Andy wryly comments, "Shazam."

When were the Darlings first seen?

The writing team of Everett Greenbaum and Jim Fritzell wrote episodes that introduced many classic Mayberry characters. Among them was their creation of a musical mountain family called the Darlings. The Darling family was headed by the widowed patriarch Briscoe Darling. Briscoe had five children, the lovely Charlene and four usually silent and usually unnamed sons.

Briscoe was played by veteran actor Denver Pyle whose last name has been said by most sources to have been used for the character of Gomer Pyle introduced earlier the same season. Charlene was played by Maggie Peterson, a young, lovely singer whom Andy Griffith's manager, Dick Linke, had seen performing at a convention for Capitol Records held in Colorado years earlier and had since begun managing.

The producers needed to find a group of actual musicians to play the four brothers as Andy Griffith wanted to include bluegrass music in the episode. As luck would have it, a young band playing at their peak musically had just been signed to Elektra Records shortly after arriving in California. Linke saw a blurb about the band's signing in *Daily Variety* and reached out to arrange an audition.

The Dillards consisted of brothers Doug Dillard on banjo and Rodney Dillard on guitar and lead vocals, with Dean Webb on mandolin and Mitch Jayne on upright bass. During their audition, the band played for Griffith, Aaron Ruben, and primary series director Bob Sweeney. They were hired on the spot. The band members had the look the producers wanted and did not have to be true actors since the characters were silent and always had blank stares on their faces.

The Darling family is first seen in "The Darlings Are Coming," which was initially broadcast on March 18, 1963. In the episode, the family came down from the mountains to meet "Private Dudley A. Wash, U.S. of A. Army, honorably discharged." Dud and Charlene were pledged in marriage to one another when they were five years old but Charlene is clearly more interested in Andy. During Andy's first encounter with the Darlings when Briscoe is filling the radiator by dipping his hat in a horse trough, the boys stand in the bed of their truck leaning on the roof of the cab while Charlene, who has been riding in the cab with her pa, gets out.

After Andy walks up to speak with them, it is clear from her behavior that Charlene is attracted to the sheriff. When Briscoe realizes this, he tells her to get back in the truck, causing her to ask, "Oh, pa. Can't I even look at the purty man?" Briscoe warns Andy "don't go makin' any fancies for her." When Andy says he has no intention of doing so, Briscoe responds, "Your words say no, but your eyes say yes."

The first time the boys' silence is played for a laugh is as the truck is preparing to pull away to go to the Mayberry Hotel. Andy gives a wave to the brothers and says, "See ya', boys." Their only response is silence and blank, emotionless stares.

Unfortunately, this scene and later ones are edited in the Paramount DVD release and the versions offered through current streaming versions. See the appendix for a description of the edited scenes from this episode. The first of the brothers to be named in the episode is the mandolin player though the name used in the filmed episode is not the name given in the script. After Briscoe pays for a single occupancy room, he smuggles his children in through the second-story window via a rope tied to the radiator. When he thinks they were all in the room, Charlene reminds him that Other (pronounced Oath-er) is still outside. Briscoe responds, "So he be. Didn't even miss him. Don't have much personality, that boy." In the script, it was not Dean Webb's character who was to have been forgotten, but rather the character played by Doug Dillard. The script also reveals Webb's character was to be named Ward. The name was changed to Other during filming as an inside joke. The makeup supervisor for *The Andy Griffith Show* was Lee Greenway. Greenway played the banjo himself and would play with the Dillards and Andy between takes. Greenway's middle name was Other so that name was used instead of Ward.

Once the Darling family are all in the hotel room, they begin rehearsing music for Charlene and Dud's wedding. Briscoe plays the jug, blowing over the top of the crock to sound notes. On the soundtrack, different notes can be heard from the jug. This was actually accomplished during the song recordings by someone blowing on different bottles filled with varying amounts of water to produce different notes.

After they are forced to leave the hotel, Andy offers to allow the family to spend the night in the cells. Aunt Bee then brings them supper. This scene is the only one in which any of the boys ever spoke on camera. As Aunt Bee collects the plates, she asks Mitch Jane's character if he had enough to eat and he responds, "About to pop." Doug Dillard's character also speaks to her but it was not as intelligible, though he was indicating the food had been good to which Aunt Bee responds with a thank you. As Aunt Bee leaves, all the boys stand and say goodnight to her. Doug Dillard's character is then named when he starts to pluck on his banjo, and Charlene warns, "Jebbin, it's 10:00 o'clock at night."

The other two brothers are not named in the episode. While not canonical, the characters were also given names in the script. Rodney Dillard's character was to be named Frankie and Mitch Jayne's was to be named Cob.

After the boys' limited speaking in "The Darlings Are Coming," they never spoke again onscreen. A running gag involved their blank, silent, emotionless faces juxtaposed with Briscoe's description of them, seemingly unaware of the unusualness of them never speaking. For example, in their second appearance in the series in "Mountain Wedding," when Andy and Barney arrive at the Darlings' cabin, after greeting Briscoe and Charlene, Andy says "howdy" to the boys whose only response is silence. Andy then says to Briscoe, "The boys are talkative today." Briscoe seems to agree, answering, "They all keyed up." Later in the episode, when Charlene comes into the room wearing her mother's wedding dress and Andy says she looks beautiful, he then looks at her brothers and says, "Don't she look pretty, boys?" The boys' expressions do not change at all and Briscoe explains, "Boys ain't much on complimentin'." (In the script for "Mountain Wedding," the name Cob was jettisoned for some reason and replaced with Ward which had been changed in the earlier episode. The four sons were to be called Frankie, Jebbin, Ward, and Other though none the character names were actually used in the episode.)

After their two appearances in the third season, The Darlings appeared twice more in the fourth (though Charlene was not in the first of these two episodes) and once in the fifth, but none of the boy's names were spoken in these subsequent episodes. The Darlings appeared for the final time in a color episode during the seventh season, "The Darling Fortune." In this episode, Andy refers to the Darling brothers by the actual names of the musicians who made up the Dillards.

While the Darling boys never spoke on camera again, they were not always silent. The fact that at least one spoke aloud though offscreen is referenced in the fifth season episode, "The Darling Baby." In the episode, Andy learns Charlene and Dud have named their baby girl Andelina in his honor as thanks for all he has done for the family. After seeing Opie, Briscoe and Charlene discuss what a nice and "mannerized" boy Opie is. Andy does not at first realize they are thinking Opie would make a good future husband for Andelina. When they ask how old Opie is and learn he is 10, Briscoe says to Charlene, "Well, uh, that ain't so bad, Charlene. Your ma was 17 when I was 30." Briscoe turned toward Andy and adds, "Of course, I was her second husband, ya' know. Her first husband got run over by a team of hogs." When the Darlings later have an engagement party to celebrate the pledging of the two children, Andy sees Barney sipping from a jug and reminds him he is on duty. Making it clear that the brothers do occasionally speak, Barney says one of the boys told him the jug only contained mulberry squeezings. Of course, Barney quickly becomes intoxicated.

While Griffith made sure the family had a certain dignity, jokes such as the one mentioned about Charlene's mother being an underaged bride did still sometimes occur. The Dillards were reluctant to play ignorant hillbillies but the roles undoubtedly brought them much wider exposure than they would have ever had without being cast on the show. Beyond question, they were among the most popular of the recurring characters and had a great impact even though they appeared in a relatively small number of episodes.

When was Ernest T. Bass first seen?

As if creating Gomer Pyle and the Darling family were not enough, Jim Fritzell and Everett Greenbaum created another beloved Mayberry character first seen in the classic episode "Mountain Wedding" which premiered on April 29, 1963.

Ernest T. Bass is an unhinged mountain man whose pursuit of Charlene Wash, Dud's new wife, brings Briscoe Darling out of the hills to ask Andy's help. Ernest T. wants to court Charlene and does not accept she is married since the ceremony was performed by Andy who is not a preacher. When Andy asks if Briscoe and his boys couldn't handle him, Briscoe responds, "Well, we thought about killin' him. Kinda' hated to go that far."

Andy and Barney go to the Darlings' cabin the next morning. Before long, Ernest T. has thrown a rock through one of the cabin windows with a note attached. To peaceably resolve the situation, Andy suggests the circuit preacher could perform another marriage ceremony. This satisfies Ernest T., who runs off cackling with laughter, saying with 24 hours before the wedding, he still has a chance.

After a long night of Ernest T. first throwing rocks through more of the cabin windows and then trying to impress Charlene by serenading her and demonstrating his ability to do his version of chin-ups, Dud yells they are having a wedding just to satisfy him. Ernest T. yells back, "You just a-think you're havin' a weddin' tomorrow. Maybe you ain't!" After he throws another rock through the window the next morning with a note threatening they will not have a bride for the wedding, Andy has Barney wear Charlene's wedding dress with a veil covering his face. During the ceremony, while Charlene hides behind a tree, Ernest T. stops the wedding by firing a shotgun into the air then grabs what he thinks is Charlene's hand and drags Barney away. The wedding is then quickly completed before Ernest T. learns the truth.

Howard Morris played Ernest T. Bass but the role was not written with him in mind. The producers had envisioned a large, lumbering man, but they were at a loss of how to cast the character. Story consultant and producer Aaron Ruben had been one of the writers on the classic Sid Caesar program *Your Show of Shows* on which Morris was one of the ensemble cast. Ruben called Morris on a hunch that he could do something with the character. When Morris read the script, he thought he had a handle on it but played the character as a heavy at first. He quickly realized Ernest T. Bass would not be funny enough if he was played as a straight heavy and so allowed his imagination to run wild.

Ernest T. often spoke in rhymes, such as saying, "You ain't heard the last of Ernest T. Bass!" Morris later said he wrote these lines himself with the producers' blessing.

Morris's take on the character was more manic than anything ever seen on the show either before or after. As a result, Ernest T. Bass had to be used sparingly so as not to overwhelm the other characters.

Morris recalled the scene in "My Fair Ernest T. Bass" where Andy and Barney have to drag him from Mrs. Wiley's. He warned Griffith and Knotts that he was really going to cling to the doorframe in any way possible and would really try to keep from being removed. Morris later recalled, "They didn't know what to do—my feet were hooking around doors—by the time they got me out of there, we were all exhausted!" The wild action in the scene definitely made it a highpoint in the series for physical comedy.

During this same period, Carl Reiner persuaded Morris to try his hand at directing. Morris made his directorial debut in a 1963 episode of *The Dick Van Dyke Show*. Morris was then invited to direct episodes of *The Andy Griffith Show*. He recalled he thought the cast was scared to death to learn the same manic actor who had played Ernest T. Bass three times previously in the series had been invited to direct on the show. Morris directed eight episodes during the fifth season. He first directed four episodes early in the season while also acting as Ernest T. in another episode directed by Alan Rafkin. Six episodes after the first batch he directed, Morris returned to direct four more episodes.

Greenbaum said the character's name of Bass came from the acclaimed graphic designer Saul Bass who did the title sequences for films such as *North by Northwest* and *Psycho*. Greenbaum's younger brother worked for Bass. The middle initial "T" was simply because he and Fritzell thought the name was funnier that way, especially when the last name was not used. Greenbaum and Fritzell had previously written for the 1950s Wally Cox series *Mr. Peepers* in which they created a school coach with the name of Frank T. Whip. They decided to use the same middle initial for the manic mountain man introduced in the episode.

When did Floyd first return after Howard McNear's stroke?

After Howard McNear left the show due to a stroke, it would obviously have been easier for the producers to either write the character out completely, recast the character, or develop a storyline introducing a new barber. The way Andy Griffith and the other producers handled the situation are a testament to the type of people they were.

The producers instead chose to keep the character present in the viewers' minds even though unseen by making references to him. For example, seven episodes after McNear's last appearance before his stroke, Hudge leads his goat into the barbershop where Andy, Mayor Stoner, and another man are sitting. When Hudge yells toward the back room to ask Floyd if he can give him a haircut, Andy explains Floyd is not in the back room but is out to lunch while they are waiting. Andy explains, "You know Floyd. Takes an hour or more. Says if he comes right back to work after eatin' it all goes down to his legs." Later that same season, Opie tries to impress Karen Burgess by casually mentioning that when Floyd gave him a haircut the previous week, he said it would not be too long before Opie was shaving.

While the character of Floyd was first played by Walter Baldwin in a single episode and then by McNear, technically an unknown actor played him a third time. The fourth season episode "A Date for Gomer" opens with a shot of Andy and Opie leaving the barbershop. A man playing Floyd is seen from a distance through the window seating another customer as Andy rhetorically asks as they walk by the barbershop window, "Why Floyd always has to get that little bit of hair down your back?"

Near the end of the fourth season, on March 16, 1964, McNear returned to *The Andy Griffith Show* in "Andy Saves Gomer." In the episode's opening scene, Andy and Floyd are sitting in the courthouse when Opie runs in, excitedly telling them he has a letter from Barney. The deputy was on a short vacation in Raleigh with his cousin, Virgil, and was living the high life. For example, they played four games of Skee-ball at the arcade in one evening. As Andy reads the letter aloud, he has to stop when he gets to Barney's description of the peekaboo blouses worn by the waitresses at a waffle shop so Opie will not hear. Opie is confused as he thought peekaboo was something you play with babies.

It had been more than 15 months since Floyd had last been seen in "Convicts-at-Large." McNear had definitely been affected by the stroke but his mannerisms were still priceless. His vocal pattern was slower than before the stroke, but it actually accentuated his already faltering speaking style and made the character all the more endearing. When McNear first returned, he had at least limited use of his left hand but as the show progressed, he was unable to use it. McNear also had trouble standing. In all four of his appearances in Season 4, he was always sitting down. In Season 5, he was most often shown sitting down and only standing a few times. Even then, he was sometimes shown noticeably leaning against a wall or doorway and not bearing his own weight.

Halfway through the season, "Otis Sues the County" aired. It was the last of eight episodes of *The Andy Griffith Show* directed by Howard Morris who also played the recurring character Ernest T. Bass. In one scene, Morris got around McNear's inability to walk well. Barney is in the back room fixing a cup of coffee for Otis. With the camera showing

Otis in the cell putting on his shoes, the sound of a door opening and Floyd's voice greeting Otis is heard. The camera then shows Barney in the back room. As he and Floyd speak to one another, the sound of footsteps are heard. When Floyd is then actually shown on camera, he is now seated. At the end of the episode, a scene called for Floyd to be cutting Andy's hair. Morris recalled, "So in the back of the barber chair we rigged up what we used to call a boatswain's seat. That's a thing that sailors use when they go up and down the mast, a piece of wood on ropes. And we tied it to the back of the chair, and it looked like he was standing. I'll never forget that I was so thrilled that he could actually do the scene. And you know what? He was, too."

McNear's health declined gradually enough that he was able to continue with the show through the next-to-last season. In "Floyd's Barbershop," county clerk Howard Sprague buys the building which houses the barbershop leading to a disagreement with Floyd over raised rent. Jack Dodson who played Howard has said it was a difficult episode to shoot due to McNear's failing health, especially since McNear was so loved by all his fellow cast members. By his final appearance in the last episode of the season, it was clear he would not be able to continue.

McNear passed away on January 3, 1969, less than a year after *The Andy Griffith Show* ended. Parley Baer who played Mayor Stoner in the series gave the eulogy at McNear's funeral. The two old friends had worked together many times, including as regulars in the radio cast of *Gunsmoke*.

When did Barney first try to resign?

Another running gag involving Deputy Barney Fife was his proclivity to tender his resignation from the sheriff's office. This first occurred early in the series. In "Andy the Matchmaker," first aired November 14, 1960, Barney feels there are no real crimes for him to solve in Mayberry and that people are making fun of him as a result. As Andy is working on the engine of the squad car parked in front of the courthouse and says hello to Barney, the deputy continues briskly walking and replies, "It ain't 'Howdy, Barney,' it's 'Goodbye, Barney.'" Andy follows him inside the courthouse to find Barney removing his badge. As he places his equipment on Andy's desk one item at a time, it includes "one bullet," which he had in his right shirt pocket as opposed to the left where he would later traditionally carry it. He instead has a whistle in his left pocket, noting he "replaced the pea in it but I ain't a' gonna' charge ya.'"

Barney explains to Andy that it is bad enough there was no "deputyin'" for him to do but he is now being teased about it, and by Opie, no less. He says he caught Opie red-handed holding chalk by the side of the bank where a limerick had been written on the wall that read:

> There once was a deputy called Fife
> Who carried a gun and a knife
> The gun was all dusty
> The knife was all rusty
> 'Cause he never caught a crook in his life

Barney argues the poem undermines the dignity of his job and laments, "If only somebody would commit a crime. One good crime! If only somebody'd just kill somebody. Oh, I don't mean anybody we know! But, well, if a couple of strangers was to come into town, and if, well, one of 'em was gonna' kill the other one anyways, he might just as well do it chere.'"

When Opie comes in and Barney insists Andy confront his son about the limerick, Opie admits to holding the chalk but said two older children had handed it to him and then ran away when they saw Barney coming. When Andy tells Opie he believes him, Barney asks if Andy is pitting his crime-detecting judgment against his. Andy explains he has to believe Opie since he knows Opie wouldn't lie to him and, more importantly, Opie has not learned to write. As Andy tries to talk Barney out of resigning and asks what Barney will do, the deputy says he might get a job at the pickle factory as they always need a brine tester. However, when Miss Rosemary, a woman Barney clearly likes, comes in and says that knowing Barney and Andy are on patrol made her feel safe, Barney quickly gives up the idea of resigning.

Later the same season, Barney attempts to resign again in "Andy Saves Barney's Morale." After Andy leaves Barney in charge as Acting Sheriff while he is away for the day then returns to discover Barney has arrested nearly two dozen people, Andy dismisses all charges while acting as Justice of the Peace. When townspeople soon begin poking fun at Barney, Andy devises a plan to pretend he is going to fire Barney since he cannot keep a deputy who is the butt of jokes. Before Andy's plan could be seen to have worked, Barney has given up on being a deputy, saying, "Why should you want a deputy sheriff that ain't nothin' but a joke?"

Just as he had previously, Barney lays his equipment on Andy's desk an item at a time, though he now carries his one bullet in his left shirt pocket as he nearly always did.

His resignation is interrupted by Aunt Bee who comes into the courthouse, locks herself in the cell, and tells Andy she was guilty of unlawful assembly, adding Mayberry is lucky to have a deputy that did his duty without showing favoritism. Soon, others of the crowd who had been arrested come back to the courthouse and voluntarily go back into the cells which puts an end to Barney's resignation.

In the second episode of the second season, "Barney's Replacement," Barney becomes convinced that a lawyer with the State Attorney's Office, Bob Rogers, who came to Mayberry and was deputized to gain practical experience in law enforcement, is actually meant as his replacement. Convinced he is going to be fired, Barney resigns, making the excuse that he had been thinking about it a while but had not wanted to leave Andy short-handed. After a less-than-successful attempt at door-to-door sales of vacuum cleaners, Barney finally stands up to Rogers and tells Andy he wants to withdraw his "retirement." In the process, Rogers learns "[t]here's a little more to sheriffing than books and charts."

In the fourth season fan-favorite episode "Citizen's Arrest," Barney resigns again. After ticketing Gomer for an illegal U-turn, Barney explains, "Now, it's from little misdemeanors that major felonies grow." He adds, "The law must be upheld. Now if I, as just plain John Doe, an ordinary citizen, were to see you making a U-turn, I'd have to make a citizen's arrest." Of course, Barney gives Gomer a ticket and then promptly makes an illegal U-turn himself. Gomer stops him and makes a citizen's arrest. As townspeople gather and back up Gomer's position, Andy arrives and makes Barney write himself a ticket in order to diffuse the situation.

Once back in the courthouse, an angry Barney feels Andy has humiliated him in front of the town. After Andy even offers to pay the $5 fine out of his own pocket to close the issue, Barney says that wouldn't close it. He refuses to allow Andy to pay the fine and does not pay it himself, saying he instead chooses to spend five days in jail, believing it will make Andy look foolish when people see Andy's ex-best friend is serving a sentence. When Andy comes into the courthouse the following morning, Barney exits the cell and hands Andy a letter of resignation. Barney stresses it is his official resignation but clearly is taken aback when Andy says he accepts it.

When Gomer learns Barney has quit, he phones in a false report of a robbery thinking it will convince Barney to come with Andy. When Andy shows up alone, Gomer says, "Funny Barney didn't come with ya'. This is a job that calls for teamwork." Gomer then admits he faked the crime to try to get Andy and Barney back together again since he is the one that caused the problem. Barney then arrives carrying a rifle after running to the filling station, apologizing to Andy for being so late and saying he came as he knew it was a job in which Andy would need somebody to cover him.

Once back at the courthouse, Barney apologizes to Andy and says he knows he made a fool of himself. Barney then asks what Andy is going to do with the letter of resignation he wrote. Andy removes it from his pocket and walks to the filing cabinet, saying, "Well, I'll tell ya', Barn. I thought I'd just, uh, file it in here with the rest of 'em." He then reads from a file previous letters of resignation dated January 21 and February 7 and is reading a third as the scene closes. Thus, in addition to the times it had happened previously in earlier episodes, there were many more resignations viewers had not seen. The fact that the two dates read aloud were sequential months gave the comedic idea that Barney resigned at least once a month over something.

When was the first time a dress being worn was pivotal to an episode's story?

Dresses were obviously seen throughout the series and sometimes were important to the storyline. While not as instrumental in the story and not really worn, the first time a dress plays a notable role was in "Ellie for Council," which premiered on December 12, 1960. A woman is frustrated she cannot charge the cost of a dress after her husband suspended their charge account to retaliate for women supporting Ellie's run for council. Upon being told she can't charge it, she takes the dress off, puts her hat on, and leaves the store in a huff in just her slip. The scene is an unusual one for the show as it is one of several in a row told in pantomime.

The first time a dress actually being worn is important to an episode is toward the end of the first season in "Ellie Saves a Female," broadcast April 17, 1961. A gruff farmer named Flint has only one child, a daughter he calls Frankie. With no sons to work as farmhands, he does not approve of cosmetics Ellie gives his daughter. After Barney is able to bring Frankie to Ellie's house without Flint knowing it, Ellie gives Frankie a makeover which includes a new dress. When she and Andy take Frankie back to the farm and Flint first sees them, he does not recognize his own daughter. Once he does, Andy asks what he thinks. He responds she is pretty but needs to get out of the dress and get back to work. He explains to Ellie that farmers with sons have built-in farmhands but that their farm was all he and Frankie have and they only have their four hands to work it. In the heartbreaking scene, Flint says, "I'd like to say, 'Thank you, ma'am, I'm mighty grateful,' but I can't. So I got to say, 'Get out of them things, Frankie.'" But Andy convinces him otherwise when he sits

Frankie on a fence and she immediately attracts the attention of the sons of Flint's neighbor. Andy points out that Frankie is only a fair farmhand but Frances is quite a girl and that if she married, Flint would gain a superior farmhand. Flint agrees. Undoubtedly, this episode is dated in its approach to women as the men discuss Frankie as if she is a piece of property that could be more effectively utilized, but the underlying sorrow Frankie's father felt is moving nonetheless.

Of course, that would be the first time a dress being worn by a woman was instrumental in a story. But what about a dress worn by a man? Barney first dons a dress in the

"She's just a beast! A beast is what she is!"

Season 2 episode, "The Bookie Barber," on April 16, 1962, when going undercover to try to prove that Bill Medwin, the new barber in Floyd's shop, is a bookie. Barney wears a dress with gloves and a hat with flowers. Before entering the the barber shop, Barney is spotted by Opie and his friend, Joey. Joey does not at first believe the person he is seeing is Barney. The boys agree Barney looks like the second-grade teacher Mrs. Cox. Once Barney enters the shop, he speaks in a falsetto and says "she" wants to place a $2 bet on a horse but has to do so quickly so "her" daughter-in-law won't find out, adding the daughter-in-law will have a fit if she does.

Dressing as a woman was a trick Barney employs again twice the following season. He first does so when trying to demonstrate the lax security at the bank in "The Bank Job." He pretends to be cleaning lady Mrs. Magruder's cousin who is filling in for her. After saying Mrs. Magruder is sick and then is asked what is wrong with her, Barney hesitates and then answers, "Fungus of the knee."

In "Mountain Wedding," the next-to-last episode of the season, Barney wore Charlene Darling's wedding dress to fool Ernest T. Bass who is determined to stop the wedding of Charlene and Dud Wash. Ernest T. disrupts the wedding and abducts who he thinks is Charlene. Once they are far from the wedding, Ernest T. says, "You're mine. You was meant to be mine. You will be mine! Charlene, I'll make you a fine husband. I'm a little mean, but I make up for it by bein' real healthy. Say you'll be mine. Say you'll be my belove-ded" Barney then lifts the veil to reveal he is not Charlene and responds, "I wouldn't marry you if you were the last man on earth!" In the epilogue, Ernest T. remains confused about the situation. He tells Dud he had better be good to Charlene and if he isn't, he will "call that lady sheriff and you'll be in real trouble." He then tries repeatedly to get Barney to dance with him.

Maggie Peterson who played Charlene later recalled that Knotts was able to wear the same wedding dress she wore in an earlier scene instead of a duplicate dress being necessary.

When was Goober first seen?

Before Goober was ever seen, Gomer Pyle had become a popular recurring character who helped take up the comedic slack after Howard McNear's stroke midway through Season 3. George Lindsey auditioned for the role of Gomer and believed he had been cast. However, when Andy Griffith discovered Jim Nabors doing his nightclub act in Santa Monica at a club called The Horn, the decision was made at the last minute to cast Nabors in the part instead.

It became clear quickly that the character of Gomer was popular with viewers. Griffith convinced story consultant and producer Aaron Ruben they needed to develop a property for Nabors or they would lose him to another network. The producers thus knew Gomer would be leaving Mayberry for his own series long before the viewers did.

In Gomer's second appearance, he refers to his cousin Goober for the first time. The writing team of Everett Greenbaum and Jim Fritzell had created yet another important character though, at the time, there was not necessarily a plan for Goober to ever be seen. Instead, the mention of Goober was at first just part of a gag. In "Man in a Hurry," first broadcast January 14, 1963, stranded businessman Malcolm Tucker asks Gomer if there isn't someone other than Wally in town who could fix his car. Goober suggests his cousin Goober. When Malcolm asks if Goober knows a lot about engines, Gomer replies, "He hopped up an old V-8 engine and put it on his rowboat. That thing'll do 80! Now, that's fast on water."

Once the show's producers knew Gomer would be leaving

Mayberry, Goober was referenced more often in anticipation of the character actually being introduced as a replacement for Gomer. For example, in the fourth season episode "Sermon for the Day," which aired October 21, 1963, visiting Dr. Breen has preached a sermon urging people to slow down, asking, "What's your hurry?" As Andy, Barney, and Aunt Bee relax on the Taylor home's front porch, Gomer walks by and is asked what he is doing. He responds, "I thought I'd run over to my cousin Goober's and watch him wash his car." After Aunt Bee says Gomer is another example of people always rushing, he joins them sitting on the porch, commenting, "Crazy. Guess I just wasn't thinkin.'"

As they relax on the porch, they soon decide to try to bring back the evening band concerts like they used to enjoy. Gomer offers to help Barney repair the bandstand and says he could borrow tools they could use. In a small inconsistency, as Gomer and Barney leave, Barney says, "C'mon, let's go see Goober," even though Gomer has not said that was whom he planned to see to borrow the tools. Apparently, there was an unseen change in plans, since when Gomer later arrives with the tools it is clear Barney has not gone with him. It is also clear the hope had been that Goober would come help with the repairs but he was only able to lend the tools.

Nine episodes later, in "Barney and the Cave Rescue," as Barney is preparing a rescue operation understandably believing Andy and Helen are trapped by a cave-in, Gomer mentions he remembers when his cousin Goober got lost in a cave while tracking a skunk. An upset Barney says he doesn't have time to hear about Gomer's "stupid cousin, Goober." Gomer then defensively adds, "My cousin Goober ain't stupid. He's ugly, but he ain't stupid."

By the time "Barney and the Cave Rescue" was aired,

the pilot episode "Gomer Pyle, U.S.M.C" had already been filmed though it would be more than four months later before it was aired as the last episode of the season.

After withdrawing the offer for George Lindsey to play Gomer, the producers kept the actor in mind as they had obviously liked what they saw. Griffith had even gone so far as to keep Lindsey on the payroll as a sort of "Southern consultant" until they could find another role. When the mountain family the Darlings were introduced, they initially offered the part of Dud Wash to Lindsey who turned it down, hoping a larger part would eventually materialize. It was a wise decision.

Lindsey was cast as Goober and was seen for the first time in "Fun Girls" which aired April 13, 1964. "Fun Girls" is one of only seven episodes written by Ruben. Lindsey said he understood immediately that, in concept, Goober was simply a copy of Gomer, so he knew he would need to work hard to make the character as different as possible.

"Well, why dontcha' do it yourself? It's easy. Well, just take the head off, clean out the input ports and the valve springs, then drain the crank case and fill it full of 40 weight. Sure, ain't nothin' to it. Okay, goodbye, Alice."

When was a temporary deputy first seen?

While Barney Fife was the deputy during the black and white years of *The Andy Griffith Show*, occasionally situations arose that called for a temporary deputy to be appointed.

While the appointment did not take place—and as was clear from the situation, was never really intended to—a temporary deputy was first mentioned in the early episode "Irresistible Andy," originally aired on October 31, 1960. In the episode, Andy invites Ellie Walker, the attractive new druggist in town, to the church picnic and dance and then becomes convinced she is trying to trap him into marriage.

Andy initially tries to get Ellie interested in other eligible men in town as possible dates. Ellie then learns what Andy has presumed. While Andy is in the drugstore, she lets him know in no uncertain terms she has no desire to marry him. She adds, "Nor do I need your generous help in getting me an escort! And just to prove it to you, I'm going to go with the first single, unattached man who comes through that door!" Barney then strolls in and is shocked when Ellie comes up and asks if he is taking anyone to the church dance. When he answers no she says she accepts his invitation, turns, and goes into the back room. The stunned deputy looks at Andy and says, "I just come in here for some foot powder." In order to trick Barney into breaking his date with Ellie, Andy later mentions he would hate to swear Jeff Pritchard in as a temporary deputy and see him get a citation for rounding up pickpockets at the church picnic and dance. Barney objects and breaks his date so he can be on duty, explaining, "I'm a deputy sheriff, not a picnicking playboy!"

The first time temporary deputies might have actually been seen is near the end of the first season in "Quiet Sam." Concerned that Andy could be in trouble at Sam Becker's house, Barney calls Floyd and tells him he needs to get Nate and Clarence and anyone else he can round up to form a posse and get to Becker's home as soon as possible. It's debatable whether Floyd had actually been deputized—Barney told him it was a civic order—but Floyd had definitely been called on to act on behalf of the sheriff's department.

The first time a temporary deputy was undoubtedly seen is early in the second season in "Barney's Replacement," originally broadcast on October 9, 1961. Bob Rogers, an attorney with the State Attorney's Office, came to Mayberry with a letter of introduction from Andy's old friend Ralph Baker. Baker has arranged for Rogers to serve as a temporary deputy as part of a plan to have his attorneys gain practical experience in law enforcement. Barney is immediately threatened by the capable temporary deputy and eventually resigns. However, Rogers' over-reliance on statistics and charts without taking the human element into account makes Barney realize Rogers is not up to the job yet, resulting in Barney rejoining the force.

After "Barney's Replacement," temporary deputies were generally played for laughs. This concept debuted in "Guest of Honor" which first aired on February 26, 1962. In anticipation of needing extra help during the Founder's Day celebration, Andy swears in Floyd the barber, Art the grocer, and hardware store owner Sam as "official temporary deputies of the Mayberry police force." Barney then says he has something to say and gives an overly-dramatic speech, saying, "Now, listen men and listen good. There's liable to be trouble out there today." He refers to them only by their badge numbers. When Art asks if they were going to be armed,

Barney says no since there will not be time to educate them in the proper use of firearms and then promptly fires his own revolver accidentally while putting it back in his holster.

Other notable temporary deputies include Otis, Gomer, and Goober. In "Deputy Otis," the last episode of Season 2, Otis had written his brother, Ralph, using the courthouse stationery. This misled Ralph into thinking Otis worked for the sheriff's office. When Otis receives a letter from Ralph at the courthouse address, he has to explain the situation to Andy. Otis says he is the black sheep of the family and never measured up to his brother in his family's eyes. Otis is dejected as his brother will obviously learn the truth since the letter revealed Ralph was coming to visit. Andy proposes actually giving Otis a temporary job to protect his ego. Barney incredulously asks, "Are you kidding? You mean you're actually gonna' give Otis a job here?" He then asks Andy what kind of job he could be given. Referring to Otis, Barney argues, "Well, he's irresponsible. He's careless. he's unreliable." Andy immediately responds he will make him a deputy.

Gomer was sworn in as a temporary deputy five times. The first time, both Gomer and Otis are sworn in without Andy's knowledge when Barney is concerned that Luke Comstock, a man Andy had been forced to shoot in the leg to stop a robbery years before, is coming back to town in "High Noon in Mayberry." Barney tells Gomer and the reluctant Otis that the three of them will need to give Andy 24-hour protection. When Barney tells them it will be a plainclothes operation, Gomer helpfully states he has a brown suit that is pretty plain.

In "The Big House," when two robbers caught by the State Police are being brought to the jail to be held, Barney reminds Andy that he has asked a number of times about getting an extra deputy. Andy agrees to let Barney find someone to serve, clearly intending whomever Barney selects to be only a temporary deputy to assist Barney during the prisoners' stay. Barney says he will find a "good, sharp candidate" then chooses Gomer, who eventually drops his rifle from the top of the courthouse three times where he is supposed to be keeping watch.

Gomer is again called into duty in "A Black Day for Mayberry" to help with crowd control when what is believed to be a gold shipment comes through town. In "Barney and the Cave Rescue," Gomer is deputized to watch the courthouse so Andy and Barney can attend a picnic with Helen and Thelma Lou. After Andy tells Gomer he will just need to answer the phone, Barney tells Gomer it is more complicated. Barney explains, "I mean, performance of your regular duties of communications, patrol coverage, watchin' out for stolen autos, and of course, cooperatin' with state and federal officials to provide for the common defense, assure domestic tranquility, and maintain law and order in the entire area." Andy then reiterates, "Mainly just answer the phone."

Finally, in "Andy's Vacation," when Barney convinces Andy to take a few days off, Gomer again serves as a temporary deputy. He has obviously done so earlier in an unseen circumstance, as Barney reminds Andy that Gomer is still sworn in from "the flood." Barney and Gomer are soon locked in a cell and yelling for help. They later come by Andy's house handcuffed together and needing to borrow an extra set of handcuff keys. By the end of the episode, in order to finally get some relaxation, Andy gives Barney a week off.

After Gomer Pyle was spun off in his own series, *Gomer Pyle-USMC*, his cousin, Goober, was soon being called upon to serve as a temporary deputy. After being introduced in "Fun Girls," the only episode of *The Andy Griffith Show* which features both Gomer and Goober, Goober is not seen again until the tenth episode of the fifth season. In that episode, "Goodbye, Sheriff Taylor," Andy considers accepting a job with Hogarth Detectives which would require him to move to Raleigh. Barney deputizes Goober, Otis, and old-timer Jud Fletcher as deputies while Andy is away. Barney tells them, based on their performance, he will pick one of them to be his permanent deputy when he takes over as sheriff.

When Barney says the three deputies need to understand why they were selected, Otis says it is because nobody else would come. Barney also administers a reflex test and throws a ripe tomato at Otis who made no attempt to catch it, resulting in it splattering all over his shirt. Later, when Andy decides not to move, Barney tells his three deputies they will each be receiving a $5 check in the mail. Otis says he should get more since he had to buy a new shirt.

While not shown doing so, both Goober and Floyd were deputized other times. In "TV or Not TV," a group of criminals come to town posing as a television production team interested in developing a television show based on the magazine article about Andy titled "Sheriff Without a Gun." When introduced to Mr. Harvey who they think is a television writer, Floyd says he was a deputy once on Veteran's Day when Andy needed someone to carry the flag in the parade. Goober says he has been deputized a couple of times during emergencies. For example, he was in charge of guarding the cannon in the park on Halloween. The kids always filled it with "orange peelings and potaters and rotten tomaters and things like that." Since he had been in charge of guarding it, they had not even gotten a grape in it. At the end of the episode, Goober and Floyd are deputized again. When Andy catches the criminals at the bank and one of them who is armed says Andy is forgetting the title "Sheriff

Without a Gun," Andy replies he doesn't carry one but his deputies do. He motions to Floyd in the front passenger seat of the squad car and Goober in back, both pointing rifles.

Goober acts as a deputy a number of other times, with the next three as a backup to Warren Ferguson, Andy's new deputy after Barney moved away. Warren first deputizes Goober to help round up women at a bazaar who are playing bingo as Warren believes it constitutes gambling. Goober even got to wear a full uniform when Andy deputizes him to help patrol the town during a Founder's Day celebration when the governor is visiting and the State Mobile Museum is on display. When Warren later deputizes Goober to help investigate Aunt Bee's missing pin, Goober wears only a cap.

In later instances, Goober basically has to beg Andy to make him a temporary deputy. The most extreme example is seen in "Suppose Andy Gets Sick." When Andy has the flu and is ordered by the doctor to get bed rest, he finally relents and appoints Goober as a temporary deputy. Goober becomes overzealous, handing out 14 traffic tickets in only one day and even crashing the squad car. Goober then "turned the deputyship over to Emmett" who also crashes the squad car after Goober had repaired it.

"Why'd you throw that tomato at me, Barn?"

When was the farther end of
Main Street first seen?

Exterior shots of downtown Mayberry and residences in town were nearly always filmed on what was known as the Forty Acres Backlot which was owned by Desilu at the time. Most of the downtown exterior shots were filmed on Main Street on the block which held the courthouse and most commonly Floyd's Barber Shop and the market. (In some early episodes, Orville Monroe's Funeral Parlor and Mortuary occupied the space which later housed the market.) These buildings and storefronts were used so frequently a replica was later built inside the studio where the show was primarily filmed.

Other buildings and businesses in the vicinity of the courthouse on the Forty Acres Backlot were also frequently seen. Directly across the street was a multi-sided building which during the first season housed a diner and then Walker's Drug Store in the storefront seen from the courthouse. The post office was across the wide street from both the courthouse and the multi-sided building. On the opposite side of the multi-sided building stood the church.

Nearly all of the "buildings" seen were actually facades consisting of walls held up by scaffolding. However, the multi-sided building and the church were enclosures with roofs.

If one exited the courthouse, turned right, and walked down the sidewalk, after the market was a small vacant lot followed by the Mayberry Hotel and then the movie theater. The farther end of Main Street on the next block was not shown as frequently. A clear shot of that block was first seen midway through the first season in "Andy Saves Barney's Morale," which premiered on February 20, 1961. In the scene, the squad car being driven by Andy pulls up alongside Hilda Mae, Barney's girlfriend, as she is walking past a coffee shop.

Hilda Mae is on the left walking in front of a coffee shop with a fire escape above. On the right of the photo behind the squad car is the mutli-sided building that housed Walker's Drugstore that season. Behind the building at the intersection, the full four-story height of the Mayberry Hotel can be seen to be taller than the surrounding buildings.

This shot is unusual as the directors generally shot the scenes with camera angles to hide the size of some of the building facades. Three-story buildings with fire escapes appeared more urban than would be expected in such an idyllic small town as Mayberry. This shot of the farther end of Main Street also allowed the audience to see the full four-story height of the Mayberry Hotel which is visible in the background. The directors were not always successful in hiding the hotel's size; it had also been clearly seen in the earlier episode "The

In a scene from "The Horse Trader," the hotel facade dwarfs the neighboring building.

Horse Trader" in the background quite literally towering above the market.

An example of how this less-seen Main Street block was usually shot came toward the end of the first season when the same coffee shop is seen in "Barney Gets His Man." The camera angle in that episode makes the storefront appear no taller than necessary. This enabled the producers of *The Andy Griffith Show* to maintain the small town feel of Mayberry while filming on a backlot that could also evoke a much larger town or city if need be depending on the camera angle used.

The same coffee shop as seen in the photo on the opposite page but shot an an angle to hide the true size of the facade.

137

When was Otis Campbell first seen?

Otis Campbell was first seen in the second episode of the series, "Manhunt" on October 10, 1960. In his first appearance, Otis is not the fully rounded character fans eventually got to know. He first refers to Andy as "Sheriff" and complains when Andy comes into the courthouse, saying it was about time he showed up. Having learned the State Police are coming, Barney is concerned they will think Mayberry is just a hick town where nothing ever happens if there are no prisoners. Barney asks Otis to stay an extra night out of civic duty so they can make a good impression. Otis replies he can't since he has choir practice that night.

As a recurring character, Hal Smith who played Otis was never under a long-term contract with the show. His first appearance could have been a one-shot but producer Aaron Ruben, the driving force behind *The Andy Griffith Show*, took Smith aside and told him, "Hal, this might develop into quite a part for you." And indeed it did. Smith played Otis as a recurring character eight more times during the first season. Over the next four black and white seasons, Otis appeared between four to seven times each season.

Otis shows more personality in his second appearance eight episodes after "Manhunt" when he advises Andy on how to deal with Ellie in the only episode in which Otis is jailed for something other than public intoxication. Just as the use of a public drunkard for humor is dated, so is Otis's expressed attitude toward women. He advises Andy to never apologize to a woman and instead to fight it out. Andy points out that is what landed Otis in jail. When Otis says his wife threw a dish at him, Andy answers Otis had swung a leg of lamb at her and accidentally hit his mother-in-law, eliciting a chuckle from Otis, who happily adds, "Yeah, right in the mouth." Regardless, Otis is a major character in this episode which allows him to be more fully developed into a "real" character and not just the basis of a single joke he had been in his first appearance.

The stock character of the town drunk who is intoxicated more than he is sober is an old one used in literature long before *The Andy Griffith Show* ever aired. Otis is used for comic relief but in Mayberry, it is also made clear those around him legitimately care about him. Andy once said, "Otis ain't a bad fella'. He's one of the nicest fellas I know. Always willin' to help out a neighbor. Generous. And for his drinkin', we don't lock him up 'cause he's botherin' anybody. It's so's he won't hurt himself."

The character's name is said to have been derived as a nod to two of Andy Griffith's friends from Mount Airy, Otis Brinkley and Keith Campbell.

When was Otis first seen intoxicated?

Casual fans often assume Otis is consistently shown to be intoxicated in the series but that is not always the case.

Otis is first seen in "Manhunt" but has already sobered up and is being released from jail. Likewise, in his second appearance eight episodes later in "Ellie for Council," a sober Otis has been jailed for "fightin' it out" when he hit his mother-in-law in the mouth with a leg of lamb.

It was not until January 30, 1961, midway through the first season, that Otis is actually shown to be intoxicated. In the seventeenth episode, "Alcohol and Old Lace," thanks to the help of the Morrison sisters, Andy and Barney congratulate themselves believing they have finally rid Mayberry of all moonshining operations. They realize they are mistaken when Otis walks into the courthouse inebriated.

After this, Otis is frequently shown intoxicated. For example, during his remaining five appearances in the first season, he is shown intoxicated in four of them.

In "Goodbye, Sheriff Taylor," Otis appears neither drunk nor in jail. He instead is one of three reluctant candidates for the position of deputy sheriff should Andy actually decide to leave Mayberry and Barney becomes sheriff.

By the mid-1960s, the show's sponsors became uncomfortable with a character who abused alcohol being used for a comic effect which resulted in less frequent appearances of Otis. During the color years, Otis appeared only once each in the sixth and seventh seasons and did not appear in the final season at all. In Otis's sole appearance in Season 6, the new deputy Warren Ferguson tells Andy he thinks Otis has a real problem. Andy acknowledges this, mentioning in the process that Monday through Friday Otis works as a glue dipper at the furniture factory. The thrust of the episode is Warren's failed attempt to cure Otis by shifting his interest to making mosaics as art. The problem is that Otis finds he does his best work when he is just a little "gassed." In the seventh season in his final appearance in the series, when Andy is held captive in a cabin and Otis and Howard Sprague plan to rescue him, Otis is not able to avoid the temptation of a bottle of whiskey Andy had confiscated from him earlier but is still able to help in Andy's rescue.

The decision was made after this to no longer use the character. To explain Otis's absence, he was referenced one last time afterward. Near the end of the seventh season, in "Opie's Most Unforgettable Character," Opie is shadowing his father while trying to do research for a writing assignment from Miss Crump. Watching Andy wipe the cell bars, Opie asks if he is expecting to lock someone up that morning. Andy says he wasn't and was just cleaning up, adding, "Since Otis started doin' his drinking in Mount Pilot, about the only customers I have are a couple of fat, old spiders."

The public's sensitivity to the effects of substance abuse has naturally only continued to increase. In the 1986 made-for-television reunion movie *Return to Mayberry*, Otis was shown to finally have his problem with alcohol abuse under control. Co-writer Harvey Bullock noted the original archetype would no longer work and recalled they got around the situation by "making him crazy about something else. So since we were putting him on the wagon, we figured we'd make him crazy about sugar. So we made him the ice cream man."

When did Otis first use the keys to the cell?

The gag of Otis being allowed to use the keys in the cell door left hanging on the wall between the cells was present from his first appearance. The concept actually pre-dated the series.

In the pilot, "Danny Meets Andy Griffith" which aired as an episode of *The Danny Thomas Show*, the town drunk is named Will Hoople. While Andy is discussing the traffic charge against Danny Williams, Will stumbles into the courthouse. He slams his fine on Andy's desk and proclaims, "I'm under arrest." Will then takes the keys to the cells off a peg in the wall. (In the pilot, the keys were kept out of reach of prisoners once in the cell instead of on the wall between the cells as they were in the series.) Will uses the key let himself into the cell. Andy explains to Danny's inquisitive wife that the situation reached the point where Andy had to arrest Will daily so he decided it would be easier to deputize him so he could just arrest himself. While the gag of the town drunk being deputized for this purpose did not carry over to *The Andy Griffith Show*, the gag of the drunk letting himself into the cell did.

Otis first appears in the second episode, "Manhunt," originally aired on October 10, 1960. While his character is not fully formed at this point, the well-known gag involving the cell keys was already in place. In the scene, Otis is sober after having spent the night in his cell. When Andy tells him his time was up, Otis reaches through the bars to remove the key ring hanging within easy reach and unlocks his cell door to let himself out. He is sometimes shown to let himself out of his cell using the keys while still incarcerated, such as was first seen on December 12, 1960, in "Ellie for Council" when Otis uses the keys to let himself out, anxious to have some of the dinner Aunt Bee brought to the courthouse. When he learns Ellie Walker has gotten 100 signatures on her petition and would be running for council, he sets his plate down and says, "I ain't hungry."

An intoxicated Otis is also sometimes shown to use the keys to unlock the cell door and let himself into his cell, but this was not seen until the end of the first season in "Bringing Up Opie" which first aired May 22, 1961. Otis had come into the courthouse intoxicated once before this, midway through the season in "Alcohol and Old Lace," but the cell door was already open in that episode so he did not need to use the keys. Otis coming into his cell with the door already open was another scenario that was repeated often.

While the character of Otis was not fully formed in "Manhunt," the gag of him using the easily accessible keys was already present.

When did Barney and Otis first yell "yeah" back and forth?

Even though Otis had already appeared 19 times over the first three seasons, the popular running gag of he and Barney angrily shouting, "Yeah?" followed by "Yeah!" at one another was not introduced until near the end of Season 3 in "Dogs, Dogs, Dogs" on April 22, 1963. In its initial incarnation, the exchanges of "yeahs" were limited to just one from Otis and one from Barney.

While eating breakfast in the cell and overhearing Barney read a letter received in response to a request from the state for additional funds, Otis asks why they need additional funds. Barney tells Otis he is one of the reasons since Andy should not have to provide meals for the prisoner. Barney says they should be getting Otis's meals from the lunch room. Otis threatens, "Well, you do that and I'll take my business someplace else!' Otis adds the food from the lunch room is too spicy. Barney argues, "You drink anything, you can eat anything!" When Otis says spicy food is bad for his liver, Barney says, "Aw, your liver's so pickled now it don't matter!" This leads to a single exchange, with Otis defiantly asking, "Yeah?" and Barney yelling, "Yeah!" Barney then repeats that Otis has a pickled liver and Otis replies it is better than having a pickled puss, which leads to another single exchange.

Later in the same episode, the gag is used again after Andy feeds part of Barney's lunch to a dog Opie has found. Otis teases Barney by asking if he has his lunches made up at a pet shop. Barney tells Otis to keep it up and he would run him in, to which Otis, still sitting in his cell, answers, "I am in!" Barney then threatens to throw Otis out, resulting in Otis asking, "Yeah?" and Barney answering, "Yeah!" The exchange continues, but instead of more "yeahs," Otis asks, "Says who?" to which Barney yells, "Says me!"

This childlike exchange of "yeahs" became a recurring gag and was expanded in future uses. For example, in the fourth season, it is first used in "Citizen's Arrest." Eight episodes later, in "Hot Rod Otis" the gag is used twice in the same episode. Barney follows an intoxicated Otis's advice about which card to play next in a game of gin rummy with Andy. The card Otis suggests turns out to be the card Andy needs. Andy lays his hand face-up and rhetorically asks, "What's the name of the game? Gin?" Otis answers, "Thank you. I don't mind if I do." An irate Barney says Otis steered him wrong and eventually tells Otis to shut up. Otis asks, "Oh, you gonna' make me?" Barney yells, "Yeah!" and Otis replies, "Yeah?" Unlike the first time the exchanges had been used in the earlier episode, they now repeat "Yeah!" and "Yeah?" several times until Andy breaks it up. The next day, after Otis is released and Andy and Barney learn Otis has bought a car, Barney decides to make Otis take a driver's test in an effort to make Otis a pedestrian again

even though he has a valid driver's license. In lieu of a written test, Barney draws an intersection on the floor of the courthouse and has Otis take a toy car while he holds another one to see how Otis will respond to various traffic situations. After Otis says he got to the intersection before Barney did, they argue until Barney tells Otis to "pipe down!" This results in another round of exchanges of "Yeah?" and "Yeah!" until Andy again breaks them up.

The gag is repeated the next season in "Otis Sues the County." The exchange is heard after Otis drags his tin cup across the cell bars. Three episodes later, it is used again when Barney doesn't like Otis being okay with having seen a bat and not a butterfly in an inkblot test administered by the deputy in "The Rehabilitation of Otis."

Once the gag was even used with a different character. When Newton Monroe comes to town and is caught peddling an hour after Andy warned him not to, Barney angrily asks if the sale was supposed to take an hour. When Newton says the customer was a careful buyer, Barney yells, "Oh, yeah?" Newton shoots back, "Yeah!" and the same exchange that always happens with Otis happens between Barney and Newton until Andy once again breaks it up.

When were Andy and Barney first referred to as cousins?

In the early episodes of *The Andy Griffith Show*, the writers and producers were still somewhat feeling their way in determining how the show would proceed. This is certainly not uncommon for any new series. The humor was broader at times and Andy Taylor was a funnier character himself before eventually settling into the straight man role surrounded by humorous characters, the first and foremost being his deputy.

The statement that Andy and Barney were cousins is an early gag, first seen in the series premiere, "The New Housekeeper" on October 3, 1960. When Barney comes to tell Andy that Aunt Bee is due to arrive soon, he says, "I want the folks in this town to realize that you picked me to be your deputy because you looked over all the candidates for the job and you judged their qualifications and their character and their ability and you come to the fair, the just, and the honest conclusion that I was the best-suited for the job—and I wanna' thank you, Cousin Andy." Andy replies, "You're welcome, Cousin Barney."

The gag was a reference to small town nepotism that leads to people getting jobs who are not truly the best qualified. But the gag is short-lived on the show. It is used again in the following episode when Barney comes to the lake and tells Andy about having received a call from the State Police about a planned manhunt. Andy says, "I never did think my own cousin could make such a fine deputy." Four episodes later, in "Runaway Kid," Barney finds the squad car in front of a fire hydrant. He comes into the courthouse and reminds Andy that Andy had told him when he was hired that an officer of the law had to uphold the law even if the person breaking it was friend or kinfolk. He then adds, "Well, Cousin Andy, operatin' on that basis, here's a citation for parkin' your vehicle in front of a fireplug." Even though "Runaway Kid" was the sixth episode aired, it was actually the fourth filmed. So using the order filmed, the gag was used in three of the first four episodes then abandoned. But even using the order the episodes were aired, the gag lasted less than two months into the show's eight-year run.

Don Knotts was not signed to a long term contract when he was first cast as Barney Fife. Series creator Sheldon Leonard later recalled, "I never knew he would become such an important element on the show." After seeing the dailies, the developed raw footage from the previous day's shooting, Leonard recognized the chemistry between Knotts and Andy Griffith and knew they needed to lock Knotts into a contract. Thus, his original purpose of being a cousin to serve as a joke was quickly abandoned.

The abandonment of the original intention to make the two characters cousins involved more than just no longer referring to it again. Andy and Barney were instead said to be old friends who had been classmates. For example, in "Banjo-Playing Deputy," the final black and white episode,

Jerry Miller, the son of an old friend of Aunt Bee's, is in town. At Aunt Bee's urging, Andy agrees to allow him to work in the courthouse for a few days, but soon decides he has to fire Jerry. When Aunt Bee objects, Andy says Jerry will end up getting himself and Andy in trouble. Aunt Bee argues, "Andy, do you mean to stand there and tell me that Barney Fife is always perfect on the job?" Andy responds, "Well, that's different. Barney's an old friend of mine."

While the original intention of the writers is clear, one can also engage in retroactively correcting the continuity by recognizing that even distant relatives or cousins once, twice, or thrice removed are often simply called "cousins" in the South. The term is also sometimes used even when there is no actual blood relation. This is even referenced once in *The Andy Griffith Show*. In the fifth season episode, "Guest in the House," Andy's attractive "cousin," Gloria, comes to stay with the Taylors after breaking her engagement. Aunt Bee constantly refers to Gloria as Andy's cousin. Before Gloria arrives, Andy complains to Helen about all the bother they are going to getting the spare room ready. Helen defends Aunt Bee, commenting to Andy that it is understandable in light of the fact that Gloria is his cousin. Andy responds, "She's not my cousin. Her mother isn't my aunt or anythin.'" Aunt Bee then says, "Oh, we've been friends for so long, it's almost like family."

When was the first time Barney was shown to carry only one bullet?

Barney is generally only allowed to carry one bullet which eventually is shown to usually be kept in his left shirt pocket. However, this is not the case the first time it was referenced.

The gag is first seen on October 10, 1960, in the second episode, "Manhunt," when the State Police are coming to Mayberry to search for an escaped prisoner. Barney expresses concern it will look bad for the State Police to arrive and find the jail cells empty. He feels better about the situation after Andy assures him they will no longer have an empty cell once they catch the escaped prisoner. Barney happily says, "Yeah, that's right! We will, won't we? Yeah, I'd better check my arms." He then pats both his shirt and pants pockets then reaches into his pants pockets, telling Andy he can't find his bullet. This exchange makes it obvious Barney is only allowed one bullet although the part of the eventual gag that he kept it in his left shirt pocket is not yet in place.

The next time Barney carrying only a single bullet is shown is five episodes later in "Andy the Matchmaker" on November 14, 1960, when Barney attempts to resign. As he lays his equipment on the desk, he reaches into his right shirt pocket and removes his bullet as he says, "One gun belt, one holster, one revolver, and one bullet." This is one of only three times Barney has his bullet in his right shirt pocket. (The other two are just before Barney enters Weaver's Department Store in "The Shoplifters" in Season 4 and when he loads his gun after seeing a flashlight in the bank at night in "TV or Not TV" in Season 5.) But for the vast majority of the times this gag is seen,

Barney keeps his bullet in his left shirt pocket. So why did he have it in a different pocket those three times?

The first time is only the second use of the still-evolving gag and Barney is shown to keep a whistle in his left shirt pocket. In the other two episodes, it is likely because Don Knotts often carried a pack of cigarettes in his left shirt pocket. The outline of a cigarette package can be clearly seen in his uniform's left pocket in a great many episodes. In the two later episodes where the bullet is in the right pocket, the cigarette pack outline in the left pocket is visible.

When did Barney first accidentally fire his gun?

The recurring gag of Barney accidentally firing his revolver is seen from nearly the beginning of the series. It is first shown in the second episode, "Manhunt" on October 10, 1960. While another common gag of Barney being allowed only one bullet is introduced at the same time but in an unrefined form, in this episode Andy allows Barney to fully load his revolver in anticipation of being called upon to help the State Police in their manhunt. After Captain Barker arrives  and is dismissive of Andy and Barney then leaves the two behind when going to set up roadblocks, Andy tells Opie the State Police are probably saving them for the big showdown. The childlike Barney immediately seizes upon the explanation. He says, "We'll be ready for

them," as he tries to pull his gun from the holster and in the process accidentally fires it. Only the sound effect of a gunshot is used.

When Barney does the same thing again during "gun drawing practice" later in the season, an effect has been added so smoke shoots out of the holster in addition to the gunshot sound effect. ("Andy and the Gentleman Crook," first aired February 27, 1961.)

Five episodes later, State Inspector Case is surprised upon inspection of Barney's revolver to find it unloaded. Though Andy explains Barney keeps his bullet in his pocket, Case tells the deputy to put the bullet in the pistol where it belongs. Barney eagerly complies and immediately accidentally fires the gun, though this time not through his holster. A gunfire flash has been added to the smoke and sound effects. ("The Inspector," April 10, 1961.)

The gag is used often throughout Barney's time on the show. Barney accidentally fires his weapon while explaining why the temporary deputies for Founder's Day will not be armed since they don't have his training. He later does the same with temporary deputy Gomer right after telling him, "If you don't know how to handle one of these things, then you got no business carrying one." He accidentally fires it at an official shooting range in Mount Pilot when he has to fulfill the annual shooting test to qualify as a deputy and when demonstrating to Thelma Lou's visiting cousin that shooting bottles is harder with a quick draw.

Barney's frequent accidental gunfire is another example of the audience's willing suspension of disbelief being necessary to enjoy the humor. Barney could have obviously accidentally shot someone or himself. When Barney first accidentally fires his revolver in "Manhunt," Opie is standing nearby, a circumstance that in "real life" would have been terrifying to Andy. In addition, Barney sometimes accidentally fires his revolver into the ceiling, such as when demonstrating how he would use the pistol to start the Boy's Day race. The Mayor's Office is sometimes shown to be on the second floor of the courthouse building yet Andy never seems worried that someone could have just been accidentally shot. Instead, the audience willingly suspends its disbelief and accepts Barney's ineptitude even with a dangerous weapon, accepting it as the running joke it is supposed to be.

Barney accidentally firing his gun into the ceiling and presumably into the room above in the episode "A Medal for Opie."

When was Clara first seen?

When the first appearance of Clara occurred is sometimes a subject of debate among fans of *The Andy Griffith Show.*

Clara was played by Hope Summers who first appeared twice near the end of the first season. She is introduced as Bertha Edwards in "Andy and Opie, Housekeepers," first aired on March 13, 1961. In the episode, Andy and Opie are less-than-stellar housekeepers while Aunt Bee is away. When they know she will be returning soon, they clean the house. When Opie says, "Boy, is she gonna' be happy when she finds out we can get along pretty good without her," Andy realizes Aunt Bee will not feel needed if she comes home to a clean house. Andy and Opie promptly make it a mess again. As they are leaving for the bus station to pick up Aunt Bee, Bee's friend comes by the Taylor home to ask when Bee will be returning. Andy refers to her as "Miss Edwards" though the Southern tradition of using "miss" in reference to an elder is common and thus would not have necessarily meant she was not married or widowed.

From the outset, the character is a busybody yet also has a good heart. The former trait is seen when, after Andy and Opie leave to pick up Aunt Bee, Miss Edwards enters the house through the unlocked front door presumably just to see what condition the house is in with Aunt Bee being away. The latter trait is demonstrated when she takes it upon herself to clean the house thoroughly to save Aunt Bee from coming home to a mess she would have to clean.

When Andy and Opie return with Aunt Bee, she has just the reaction Andy had feared when she comes into the clean living room. Unaware of how the house became clean and without Aunt Bee hearing, Andy tells Opie to go upstairs and make a mess of his room. When Aunt Bee goes up to Opie's room after hearing him making noise, Andy goes into the kitchen to make it a mess again. When she then comes into the kitchen and thinks Andy is trying to hurriedly clean so she would not see the mess. The result is Aunt Bee once again feels needed. In the epilogue, when Miss Edwards drops by later, Bee calls her "Bertha." When Bertha expectantly asks how the house looked when Bee returned, she is offended when Aunt Bee answers, "Oh, Bertha, you wouldn't believe it. It looked as if it hadn't seen a dust mop or a broom since the day I left." When Bertha expresses surprise, Aunt Bee adds, "Oh, worse. It looked as if it had been taken care of by somebody who would be more at home in a pigpen."

Bertha appeared again five episodes later as a customer at a rummage sale to raise money for the Scoby family who was being foreclosed upon by the skinflint Ben Weaver. These were the only two appearances of the character played by Hope Summers during the inaugural season.

In only the second episode of Season 2, Summers appears in an episode again in "Barney's Replacement" on October 9, 1961, but she is now called Clara, the first name of the character from that point on through the rest of the series. Her last name is not given in the episode.

Clara was a recurring character who did not appear that often during the black and white seasons. After her appearance early in the second season, she appears only three more times during the season. In the fan-favorite episode "The Pickle Story" which first aired on December 18, 1961, it is clear she is a friend of Aunt Bee's. When Clara professes not to be an expert at making pickles,

Aunt Bee calls her by her full name when she says, "Oh, Clara Johnson, you are. Anyone who wins the blue ribbon at the fair for ten years in a row?" Clara corrects her that it is eleven years. She remains Clara Johnson the rest of the season and for the third and fourth seasons as well.

Some argue that Bertha Edwards was simply a different character than Clara Johnson who was just played by the same actress. This was not an uncommon occurrence on periodic television at the time. However, Hope's character was always a close and good friend of Aunt Bee's who also had a tendency to meddle. Thus, most Mayberry fans assume she was the same character and just underwent a name change, possibly because the writers simply forgot the character's name. This happened on the show occasionally. The bandleader of Bobby Fleet and his Band with a Beat became Freddy Fleet in a later season. Chronic jaywalker and hypochondriac Emma was consistently called Emma Brand until her final episode when she was instead called Emma Watson.

Clara appears only once during the third season, twice during the fourth, and thrice during the fifth. In her only third season episode, Andy calls Clara "Miss Johnson." In her two fourth season appearances, Clara's last name is still Johnson. Reverend Tucker introduces her by that name in "The Sermon for the Day" and grocer Mr. Foley calls her "Mrs. Johnson" in "Bargain Day." (The character was a widow, which may explain why Foley said "Mrs.") Up to this point, the end credits simply listed Hope Summers' name.

In the fifth season, while her first name remains Clara, her last name changes bacck to Edwards, the same last name she first had when she was Bertha during the first season. The use of the last name of Edwards for the character was originally an inside nod to the maiden name of Andy Griffith's wife, the former Barbara Edwards. The likely explanation is that the name change was made again as another nod to Griffith's wife's maiden name. Some fans explain the name change by saying that "Edwards" was Clara's maiden name while "Johnson" was her married name and that, for whatever reason, she reverted back to her maiden name at this point. Regardless, she was Clara Edwards for the rest of the series.

In the first of her three episodes during the fifth season, the character is not only called Clara Edwards by John Masters when discussing that she would be playing Lady Mayberry in the Founder's Day Pageant, the credits even listed Hope Summers as playing "Clara Edwards." Toward the end of the season in her second appearance that year in "Aunt Bee's Invisible Beau," the character is listed in the credits by her first name only as simply "Clara."

In her final appearance during the last black and white episode, Andy again calls her Miss Edwards. She is clearly meant to be the same character but the credits instead list Hope Summers as playing "Miss Bedloe." The script called for one of the two women who complained about the carnival show to be Miss Bedloe. Since Hope Summers was available, the character was changed to Clara Edwards with the character name mistakenly not corrected in the credits.

With the loss of Don Knotts who left the series at the end of the fifth season, the characters of Goober and Floyd were used even more heavily to pick up more of the comedic slack. Likewise, with more room in the stories without Barney, Clara Edwards was seen more frequently than she had been during the first five seasons. She appeared in seven episodes each during the sixth and seventh seasons and half a dozen times during the eighth and final season.

When was the first time someone was shown smoking?

When *The Andy Griffith Show* premiered in 1960, smoking was far more accepted than it is today. A decade later, while characters could still be shown smoking, Congress passed a public health act that banned the advertising of cigarettes on television and radio.

The first instance of smoking is seen in the pilot, "Danny Meets Andy Griffith" (February 15, 1960). Danny Williams has an unlit cigar in his hand from the first moment he is seen, but the first character to actually smoke is hand-me-down store owner Mr. Johnson played by Will Wright who would later play Ben Weaver in Mayberry. He smokes a cigar while Andy convinces him to settle the matter with the widow Perkins about the suit in which her deceased husband was buried. The first person with a lit cigarette is also in the pilot. TV show host Ted Parker smokes while conducting a remote interview of Danny who is being held in the Mayberry Jail.

In the ongoing series, the first person to be seen smoking is a townsman smoking a pipe before the State Police arrived for a manhunt in the second episode, "Manhunt," originally aired on October 10, 1960.

The first person to smoke a cigarette in the series is seen in the following episode, "The Guitar Player," which originally aired on October 17, 1960. Bandleader Bobby Fleet not only smokes but does so while in the jail cell. The first character to be seen actually smoking a cigar in the series is "Gentleman" Dan Caldwell in the episode "Andy and the Gentleman Crook," which aired February 27, 1961.

He does so while telling an enthralled Opie—and Barney—the story of how "Babyface" Nelson broke out of jail.

It was not uncommon to see other characters smoking. For example, while he is only shown smoking once, Otis is a smoker. In "Wedding Bells for Aunt Bee," while picking up his suit from the cleaners, Otis sees shop owner Fred Goss trying to convince Aunt Bee to go to a dance with him. Knowing he would be in jail that night after drinking, Otis brings his suit to leave in the cell to change into in case he is released in time for church on Sunday. He lights a cigarette while telling Andy about seeing Goss asking Aunt Bee for a date.

While this is the only time Otis is shown to smoke, it is not the only time it was referenced. Three seasons later in "The Rehabilitation of Otis" after Barney arrests and handcuffs Otis, Otis is offended and upset. After he sobers up, Otis remains angry about the arrest and says he is never coming back to the Mayberry Jail again. After Andy and Barney learn Otis has decided to throw all his business to the Mount Pilot Jail and they are not able to convince him to return, Barney says he really misses him. The deputy sadly takes Otis's robe off the coat tree in the courthouse. He suggests they box up the robe and send it to Otis in Mount Pilot, then suggests they also put some cigarettes in with the robe. By the way, Otis's cellmate in the Mount Pilot Jail, Luke, was played by Frank Cady who played the town drunk in the pilot episode for *The Andy Griffith Show*.

Speaking of Fred Goss, the character is a prime example of smoking used in the show as a gag. As Fred comes from the back room of his cleaning shop with Otis's suit, he tells Otis he was able to get the spots out but adds, "It might save us all a lot of trouble if you'd just get yourself a whiskey-colored suit." As the owner of the cleaning shop is telling this to

Otis, he brushes ash off his own vest which has obviously dropped from the long column of ash hanging from the cigarette dangling from his mouth. As Fred speaks to Aunt Bee, he flicks ash off his cigarette and onto Otis's suit he is carrying while saying, "It always pays to look your best." When he flicks ash onto the suit a second time, Otis reaches to try to take the suit from Fred, saying with concern, "My suit!" Mistaking Otis's concern, Fred looks down at the suit and says, "Oh, yeah, you're right. It needs cleanin' bad."

A notable example of a whimsical use of a character smoking is found in the opening episode of the third season, "Mr. McBeevee." In that classic episode, the title character not only smokes, but also shows Opie how he can make it look as if he is blowing smoke out of his ears.

When was Andy first seen smoking?

Just as secondary and background characters are shown smoking, Sheriff Taylor is shown to smoke at times as well.

Offscreen, many of the actors on the show smoked which certainly included Andy Griffith. However, Sheriff Andy Taylor was not seen to smoke in an episode until near the end of the first season. After being called upon to handle the stressful emergency of delivering Lily Becker's baby unassisted in "Quiet Sam," first seen May 1, 1961, Andy is relieved after everything has gone well. After placing the newborn in his father's arms, Andy says, "Let's go outdoors, Barney. I could use a smoke." This was an ad lib. The script just had Andy saying he could use some fresh air. On the porch, Andy removes a cigarette from his left shirt pocket and smokes it briefly until he notices the posse Barney has organized, led by Floyd who is armed with only a rock.

After smoking just a single time in the first season, Andy smokes seven times during the second season with nearly all of them in the latter half. In the tenth episode, "The Clubmen," as Andy and his friend and Esquire Club member Roger Courtney pull up to the courthouse at the beginning of the episode, Andy has a cigarette in his hand which he puts out after he gets out of the car. Eight episodes later, early in the second half of the season, Andy smokes again in "Jailbreak." Eight more episodes later, beginning with the 26th episode, "Wedding Bells for Aunt Bee," Andy smokes in five of six episodes in a row. Thus, during Season 2, Andy smokes in more than 20% of the episodes.

Andy also smokes intermittently throughout the third

season, beginning with the opening episode, "Mr. McBeevee." He smokes four more times throughout the season, with the last being "The Great Filling Station Robbery" which aired February 25, 1963.

During the fourth season, the incidence of Andy smoking drastically lowers, though the first time he is shown smoking is more shocking than any other time in the series. In "Gomer the House Guest," while Gomer is staying with the Taylors for a short time, Andy is repeatedly awoken due to Gomer making noise late at night. When Gomer is singing about a "no account mule," Andy is actually smoking in bed, an extremely dangerous practice.

The following and final instance of Andy smoking was later in the same season in "Prisoner of Love" when he smokes on his front porch while contemplating going back to the jail where an attractive female prisoner is being held.

On January 11, 1964, the Surgeon General of the United States released a landmark report warning that cigarettes were a cause of lung cancer and likely heart disease and urged the government to act. "Prisoner of Love" aired on February 10, 1964 but was actually filmed shortly before the Surgeon General's announcement. Following the report, Andy is no longer shown to be a regular smoker.

Because the depictions of his smoking are often fleeting, and sometimes especially fleeting as in the case of "The Clubmen," casual fans are often surprised to find Andy smoked more than a couple of times. In fact, from the first time Andy is shown smoking late in the first season through the last time midway through the fourth season, he is shown smoking in just under 18% of the episodes.

When was Barney first seen smoking?

Just like Andy Griffith and many others, Don Knotts also smoked offscreen. The clear outline of a cigarette package could often be seen in his left shirt pocket which supposedly only held a single bullet in the running gag.

In one episode, an actual open pack of Knotts' cigarettes could be briefly seen in Barney's open shirt pocket. In the fifth season episode, "Barney's Physical," Barney is out of uniform while being fed to excess by Aunt Bee in an attempt to get his weight up due to new physical requirements for deputies. As he tries unsuccessfully to eat one last bite, the camera pans to follow the fork as it leaves the plate. An open pack of Knotts' cigarettes is briefly visible in his left shirt pocket since Barney's civilian shirt does not have a flap covering it like the left pocket of the deputy uniform does.

While Knotts may have smoked, the character of Barney Fife was not adept at smoking, at least when it came to cigarettes. The first and only time Barney is shown smoking was in "Citizen's Arrest" which originally aired December 16, 1963. After Gomer made a citizen's arrest of Barney for making an illegal U-turn, Barney resigns and defiantly chooses to serve his time in jail to make a point rather than pay the fine or even allow Andy to pay if for him. When Andy comes back that evening, he finds Barney standing in the cell with a lit cigarette in his hand. Barney then puts the cigarette in his mouth and marks off the date on a calendar in the cell, indicating he has served his first day.

When Andy comes to the cell and comments on Barney smoking. Barney takes quick, small puffs on the cigarette, then says, "That's right. I'm smokin'. What's the matter? Smokin' lamp out or somethin'?" He continues to try to talk like a hardened prisoner, adding, "What'd ya' come back for? Bed check? Okay, take a look, screw." Barney lifts the mattress on the cot in the cell and says there were no weapons or saws. He comes back to the cell bars and says everything is a-okay, then puffs again but comically chokes a bit on the smoke this time. After Andy tells him he can stay in the cell if he wants to, Barney takes a long draw of smoke and coughs harder with his eyes bugged out in Knotts' trademark manner.

Barney is shown with cigars on three occasions but in the first two, they are unlit. In the first season episode "Mayberry on Record," originally aired January 19, 1961, Barney and some others in town invest in Mr. Maxwell's recording venture. After learning the album *Music from Mayberry* is a success and he will be getting dividend checks, Barney is sitting in the courthouse with his feet up and reading *The Wall Street Journal*. When he lowers the newspaper, an unlit cigar is clenched between his teeth.

In the second season episode "The Clubmen," Barney is sure he and Andy will be invited to join the exclusive Esquire Club. In the back room of the courthouse, he describes the club as important and says, "Just think, Andy. Today, a couple o' unknown boys in a small-town sheriff's office. Tomorrow night, members of the Esquire Club." When Andy points out they are not in it yet, Barney says they will be. As Andy asks what makes him so sure, Barney reaches in his left shirt pocket, produces a cigar, and confidently says, "'Cause we're the Esquire types." He then puts the unlit cigar in his mouth and walks out of the room.

Finally, in the fifth season episode "If I Had a 1/4 Million," Barney finds a suitcase filled with cash. Believing the criminal who abandoned the suitcase will come back to town to look for it, Barney wants to serve as "bait" by pretending to be "somebody throwing around fresh money." Against Andy's wishes and without his knowledge, Barney puts on his salt and pepper suit and is soon strolling down Main Street smoking a cigar. He lets it be known to Floyd he is thinking of taking a bus to Florida to bet $200 on horse races then gives Floyd a cigar. Floyd is impressed by the smell of the cigar and Barney explains, "Thirty-five cents a copy."

While Barney is not seen smoking a cigar in the episode, near the end of the second season in "Andy on Trial," Andy goes to a large city to arrest publisher J. Howard Johnson for failure to appear for a traffic ticket. When first speaking to Andy, Johnson offers him a cigar. Andy turns it down and then reconsiders and takes one for Barney. He tells Johnson, "Oh, maybe I will take one for my deputy. He likes one when he's feelin' special sporty."

When was the Mayberry Courthouse and Jail first seen?

A version of the Mayberry Courthouse and Jail is first seen on February 15, 1960, in the pilot episode "Danny Meets Andy Griffith" which aired as an episode of *The Danny Thomas Show*. The exterior is seen as Andy pulls up in the squad car followed by Danny Williams and his family in their car. After they enter, the interior has the same general layout as is eventually seen in the series but with differences, such as a window on the back wall.

Andy has a desk in the courthouse which also serves as his bench when presiding as a justice of the peace. In the pilot, he uses a "writing desk" with four legs and drawers under the writing surface that resembles a table. The desk has two phones which were a more contemporary style with the microphone and receiver in handsets. The desk also has a sign reading "Sheriff." A separate "Justice of the Peace" sign is substituted for it when Andy changes the official capacity in which he is acting.

In *The Andy Griffith Show*, the exterior of the courthouse was literally the subject of the first shot in "The New Housekeeper" which premiered October 3, 1960. The interior is the setting for the first scene in which Andy as Justice of the Peace performs the wedding between Rose and Wilbur. Andy's desk is now a pedestal desk with stacks of drawers on either side when seated. The desk has a single candlestick telephone. In the ongoing series, Andy has a sign on his desk reading "Sheriff" on one side and "Justice of the Peace" on the other so he just has to turn the sign around when changing the position he is fulfilling at the time. While the courthouse generally looks as it would for the rest of the series, there are differences during the first season. From the outside, the courthouse has large windows flanking both sides of the double doors that lead into the building. But during the first season, the wall to the left of the door as one enters is solid with the window inexplicably missing on the inside. Beginning with the second season, a window is shown in the interior shots.

Windows flanked the courthouse doors in the facade on the Forty Acres Backlot.

There is a door in the corner to the left when facing the cells which is incongruous. Fans sometimes jokingly refer to it as the "door to nowhere." The door disappears after the first season. Across the room on the wall beside the entrance to the back room, a radiator sits below the bulletin board during the first season. Beginning with the second season, the radiator is gone and a heater sits in the corner where the "door to nowhere" used to be. However, the courthouse is sometimes heated by gas and sometimes by coal, depending on the needs of the particular story.

In scenes set inside the courthouse during the first season, when the door was open or a view could be seen through the window, the "buildings" across the street did not match the building facades which were actually across

A interior window was missing during the first season. The "door to nowhere" disappeared after this season and was replaced with a heater in the corner.

the street from the courthouse facade on the backlot. This was because the interior scenes were shot on a soundstage with a fabric backdrop to represent the exterior. The show at first used a random, generic backdrop. In the hiatus between the first two seasons, a new backdrop was prepared that accurately depicted the view one would have on the backlot if looking out from the courthouse.

Just as in all television, the audience's suspension of disbelief allows such inconsistencies to pass. In fact, there is an even larger inconsistency fans willingly ignore. In the wall to the left as one enters the courthouse (the wall that constituted the back walls of the cells), one cell has a window. In the first season episode, "Christmas Story," an alley which is entered from the direction of the street is first shown to be on the other side of the wall. However, that wall would actually be the wall between the jail and Floyd's Barber Shop. Exterior shots show there could not be an alley there.

When was Mayberry being in
North Carolina first made clear?

Even the most casual of fans would instantly answer that Mayberry is located in North Carolina, but it took years for that fact to be officially acknowledged on the show.

Early in the series, show creator Sheldon Leonard thought it would be better for the town to simply be situated in the generic South without a specific state being identified. Andy Griffith felt it should not be an issue to state Mayberry was in North Carolina. Griffith later recalled, "At first, Sheldon didn't want it to be in North Carolina. He just wanted it to be somewhere in the South. And I hate these made-up names. So we did have Mount Pilot which there is a place called Pilot Mountain up near Mount Airy. But I gradually started slipping in real towns in North Carolina like Asheville and Raleigh and Siler City. And so it became, during that first year, it became a town in North Carolina."

Griffith's recollection is arguably correct but it was not specifically stated to be so that quickly. Raleigh is referenced during the first season, from being where Rose Blake went to get her new set of dentures to Jim Lindsey's hit record "Rock and Roll Rosie from Raleigh." Yet it is never identified as the same Raleigh that is the capital of North Carolina. In "Andy and the Gentleman Crook" which aired on February 27, 1961, during the first season, the State Police are headquartered simply in "the capital" with no reference to Raleigh. A year later, in the second season episode "Andy and Barney in the Big City," first seen March 26, 1962, Andy and Barney travel to "Capital City" instead of Raleigh to meet with the head of the State Budget

Committee for Sheriff Departments to request additional funding. (The stock footage shown to represent Capital City was of Seattle, Washington!) Nearly another year later, when the state governor's car is ticketed by Barney for a parking violation in "Barney and the Governor" (January 7, 1963), the license plate had been altered so it read "Noth Capolnja."

While references to real cities in North Carolina are made early in the series, the first specific confirmation that Mayberry was in the Tarheel State was seen in the fourth season episode, "Prisoner of Love," aired on April 18, 1964. When a beautiful, unnamed prisoner is to be held temporarily in the jail, she is brought by officers with arm badges on their uniforms which clearly read "North Carolina."

While not the highest resolution, the badge clearly reads "North Carolina Highway Patrol." This was also the first time the uniform shown for a state officer matched the actual uniforms worn in North Carolina.

The next season, in "Aunt Bee's Romance," which first aired October 19, 1964, Bee receives a letter from Roger Hanover with an address that is partially obstructed but presumably reads "Miss Beatrice Taylor, Mayberry, North Carolina."

It was not until the sixth season, the first in color, that the words "North Carolina" are finally said aloud. In "The Taylors in Hollywood," Andy, Opie, and Aunt Bee travel to Hollywood where the film *Sheriff Without a Gun* is being made based loosely—*very* loosely—on Andy's career as a sheriff. After they arrive, they are riding a bus on the way to the hotel when Opie comments he saw another "grown-up lady in trousers." Aunt Bee adds the woman was also wearing gold shoes, prompting Andy to comment it seems all right here but he would hate to see it in Mayberry. A bus driver who had just gotten off duty is sitting behind them and overhears the conversation. He asks, "Mayberry? You folks aren't from Mayberry, North Carolina?" It turns out he is from Ruby Creek, evidently another town in North Carolina.

When was the Taylor home first seen?

Not surprisingly, the first interior rooms of the Taylor home are seen in the series premiere, "The New Housekeeper." As much of the episode occurs in the home, several rooms are shown. The first to be seen is the kitchen.

The kitchen appears as it generally always does during the black and white years, though small cosmetic changes are shown from time to time in all the rooms over the course of the series. Just like the courthouse interior set, the Taylor home sets changed at times. During the black and white years, the kitchen has a backdoor in the same wall as the sink. In the color years, the door has moved and is instead in the perpendicular wall beside the hutch.

In the premier episode, as Andy tries to explain to Opie how important it is that they accept Aunt Bee into their lives, they hear a knock at the front door. (It was never explained exactly how Aunt Bee got to the house.) The next room to be seen was the living room. As Andy and Opie walk into the room, a raised

The picture originally believed to be of a young Frances Bavier hangs on the wall above the platform.

platform is in front of the door, causing one to have to step up to be level with the front door. The platform appears in this first episode and then is never seen again.

Other variations last longer before changing. In "The New Housekeeper," a set of French doors are seen to the left of the fireplace in the living room. (The doors were more visible in later episodes during the season.)

By the second season, the doors are gone and a window is instead in their place. During the first season, a mounted deer head hangs above the fireplace. Beginning in the second season, a print of the famous painting "The Angelus" hangs there instead. Finally, during the first two seasons of the series,

French doors were seen during the first season.

if one walks through the front door, a solid wall is seen immediately to the left. By the third season, a coat closet is instead in that wall, which is fortunate since this is where Barney discovers Colonel Harvey's Indian Elixir on the closet shelf and later uses as a good spot to stretch his height to meet the new

A window was seen beginningin the second season.

requirements for deputies by the Civil Service Office.

Opie's bedroom is the next room seen in "The New Housekeeper." After Opie says he does not like the fried chicken as prepared by Aunt Bee, Andy tells him to go to his room, not initially seeing the child fill his plate with food to take with him. The audience learns Opie's room is upstairs when Andy tells him, "Since you're not gonna' eat anything, you might as well go on up to your room."

While minor set dressing changes are later seen, the main difference in Opie's bedroom from later appearances is that Opie has a birdcage on a stand by his window where his pet bird, Dickie, is kept. After the episode, the cage and Dickie disappear. One odd change in the set dressing is seen from one scene to the next in this episode. Initially, Opie has a globe on the nightstand by his bed. In the same episode in the next scene in his room, a lamp with a ceramic lamb as the base has replaced the globe.

Opie's room being upstairs is confirmed at the end of the episode when he looks down from his window to see Andy preparing to take Aunt Bee away in a truck that was also never seen again. Perhaps Andy borrowed it.

It would be some time before various other rooms of the house were shown. While much of the interior of the Taylor home is seen in "The New Housekeeper," the exterior is not seen other than the unattached garage. In the scene where Opie says he won't love Aunt Bee and Barney then comes to let Andy know that Aunt Bee will be arriving the next day, Andy is waxing the squad car at his home with the garage in the background. However, it is not the same garage seen in the rest of the series.

The exterior of the Taylor home sat on a "residential street"

A different garage was seen in the first episode. Note the angled boards in the door panels.

in the Forty Acres Backlot owned at the time by Desilu. What appeared to be actual "houses" were really just facades without a roof or rear walls. In "The New Housekeeper," the garage as shown would have to be to the left of the unseen Taylor home since no house is visible to the left of the garage. This was the only time the garage is shown to be in that location, the reason being that the producers had not yet decided on which facade to use for the Taylor home. Assistant Director Bruce Bilson, who was the Assistant Director for the first two seasons of *The Andy Griffith Show*, has said he does not recall the location used for the garage in "The New Housekeeper." It does not appear to have been on the Forty Acres Backlot.

No portion of the house exterior itself is seen until the fifth episode, "Irresistible Andy," which originally aired on October 31, 1960. The front porch is first seen as Andy sulks after realizing he has been foolish in thinking Ellie Walker was trying to land him as a husband. While this episode is the first time the public sees the house exterior, this is only because of the variation between the order of filming and airing. "Irresistible Andy" was the fifth episode of the series to air but it was actually the seventh filmed. The episode "Runaway Kid" also included a front porch scene and was filmed before

"Irresistible Andy" but was aired later as the sixth episode.

In scenes on the front porch, a trellis is shown on the side opposite the set of porch steps. The backlot street had only a few house facades which often had to pull double duty to serve as different homes. When the facade is meant to represent the Taylor home, the trellis is normally attached to the end of the porch. When the facade is meant to represent a nondescript house, the trellis is missing.

The Taylor front porch continues to be seen frequently but a wider shot that shows the whole house is not seen for quite some time. The first instance of being able to see the entire facade was in a scene where the facade was not meant to represent the Taylor home. In "Christmas Story," which first aired on December 19, 1960, humbug store owner Ben Weaver sees the squad car driving down the residential street with the facade visible in the background but without the trellis. (The garage still could not be seen due to the camera angle.) Two episodes later, in "Mayberry Goes Hollywood," the house can again be seen in the background but is again missing the trellis which the Taylor front porch had been shown to have. This is also the first time the second floor could be clearly seen to have a single set of windows in the center facing the street.

A good example of why the trellis distinction was necessary due to the limited number of house facades can be seen in "Andy's Rich Girlfriend." When Andy drives to see Nurse Peggy, on the Forty Acre Backlot, her house is only two doors down from the facade that served as Andy's house which was plainly visible in the background. The missing trellis makes it appear to be a house other than Andy's.

Occasionally, though rarely, the porch trellis is missing

Peggy's new convertible is parked in front of her house which could be seen as the camera panned to follow Andy walking to her door. Since it was just two doors down from the Taylor home, the trellis is absent on the Taylor facade to allow it to appear to be a different house.

even when the facade is meant to be the Taylor home. This is first seen in "Aunt Bee's Medicine Man" when Andy arrives home to hear a rousing rendition of "Chinatown, My Chinatown" being sung by Aunt Bee and the Ladies Aid Church Committee from the street.

A view of the entire facade of the Taylor home is not seen until the final episode of the first season in "Bringing Up Opie," originally aired on May 22, 1961. Opie is sent outside to plant two rows of spinach by Aunt Bee who says it will be educational for him to eventually see the plants growing right before his very eyes. Opie argues in vain, "But spinach? Couldn't I see something else grow up before my very eyes?" Later, when Opie is watering the spinach seeds, the entire facade, including the garage to the right of the house, is finally seen. The garage door is made of

Randy Turner

The garage to the right of the house as normally seen.
Note the door is made of vertical boards.

vertical boards and not the angled boards as had been shown in the series' first episode, "The New Housekeeper."

The exterior underwent one other major change. During the first three seasons, the second floor had only a single set of windows facing the street (as seen in the photo on the facing page). Beginning the next season, the facade instead has two separate windows.

When were bedrooms in the Taylor home first seen?

As previously discussed, Opie's upstairs bedroom is seen in the first episode. Other than Opie's room, another bedroom in the Taylor home is not seen until the first episode of the second season which aired on October 2, 1961. In "Opie and the Bully," Opie comes to Andy to leave a change of clothes which he thinks he might need since he plans to stand up to the bully, Sheldon, who has been taking his milk money. Andy's bedroom is shown to have a second door that opens up to the outside. Since Andy is always shown to go upstairs at bedtime, the door presumably opens onto a balcony. Tree branches are seen alongside the balcony wall. A window in his room also overlooked the balcony. The room would have to have been on the back of the house since the front and sides of the house were sometimes seen and no balcony is visible. Near the end of the third season, Andy's bedroom has the same general layout although the door outside is closed when the visiting

gentleman's gentleman Malcolm Merriweather is trying to help Andy put on his pants much to Andy's dismay.

Like so many other instances though, the bedroom location changes to fit the needs of the particular episode. Early in the fourth season, in "Gomer, the House Guest," Andy's bedroom does not have a doorway to the outside and actually faces the street even though previously it was Opie's room which did so. (As noted earlier, the facade of the home on the Forty Acres Backlot had been altered to now have two windows facing the street instead of the single window seen during the first three seasons.)

Aunt Bee's room is first seen in "High Noon in Mayberry" midway through the third season when she is awakened by the reluctantly deputized Otis prowling around outside the Taylor home while keeping watch for Luke Comstock, a man Andy had shot in the leg in the line of duty years earlier and whom Barney is convinced is returning to Mayberry to do Andy harm.

In a sense, both Andy's and Aunt Bee's rooms are seen in "The Rumor" at the end of the fourth season. Andy's room has returned to having a door to the outside in this episode. The room is redecorated to make it suitable for Helen on the mistaken rumor spread by Barney that Andy and Helen are to be married. When the truth is learned, Andy gives the room to Aunt Bee and takes her room instead.

When was a spare bedroom in the Taylor home first seen?

The question of whether the Taylor home has a spare room varies depending on the needs of the particular episode.

A spare room is implied to exist in "Aunt Bee's Brief Encounter," first aired early in the second season on December 4, 1961, when Aunt Bee insists "handyman" Henry Wheeler stay inside the house instead of sleeping in his truck.

A spare room is first shown in another second season episode, "Aunt Bee, the Warden," aired March 12, 1962. In the episode, since the cells are full at the jail, Otis is taken by Andy to the Taylor home to serve his sentence under the stern and watchful eye of Aunt Bee. Andy tells Aunt Bee he is going to put Otis in their guest room. Otis first has a taste of what he is in for when Aunt Bee brings a breakfast tray the next morning and speaks to him through the door. Otis tells her to keep it hot so he can sleep in a bit longer. When Aunt Bee tells him he will eat then or not eat at all, he says, "Now just a minute! I got my rights. I'm a prisoner in this house, and I expect to be treated like one." She then comes into the spare room and, when he still fails to get up, dumps water from a flower vase onto his head. When Aunt Bee puts him to work as a prisoner and foils his attempts to escape, Otis comes to call her "Bloody Mary" and refers to Andy's house as "The Rock."

Yet in the third season episode "Man in a Hurry," the house has no spare room. Opie is disappointed when he learns the stranded Malcolm Tucker will not be spending the night with them after all. He tells Mr. Tucker he was looking forward to sleeping on the ironing board suspended between two chairs.

When Malcolm says that sounds terrible, Opie responds, "No, it ain't. That's adventure-sleepin'!" But ten episodes later, the implication is that Malcolm Merrieweather stays in a spare room while working off a debt in "Andy's English Valet." (While he could have been staying in Aunt Bee's room while she was away, during his next visit the following season he again stays with the Taylor's while Aunt Bee is home.)

In "Gomer, the House Guest" which aired early in the fourth season, a spare room is again seen and is shown to adjoin Andy's bedroom. Both rooms overlook the street. (The producers took advantage of the change to the house facade discussed previously.) When Gomer is fired from his job at Wally's Filling Station, he loses his residence since he normally stays in the back of the garage. Andy invites Gomer to stay with him until he finds a new job. He soon comes to regret his generosity as Gomer makes excessive noise which keeps Andy from sleeping. After Gomer wakes the family at 2:30 in the morning trying to repair their vacuum cleaner, and Andy finally convinces Gomer to go to bed, Gomer comments, "Ya' know, Andy, for a man that's gotta' get up so early in the mornin', you sure do keep strange hours."

The next day, Andy explains to Gomer that he had made so much noise he kept Andy awake. Gomer apologizes. While Gomer tries to be quiet that night, word has spread that he is staying at Andy's. As a result, townsmen bring their cars by the Taylor home, pulling up in the street in front of the house and shouting to get Gomer's opinion on what was wrong with their vehicles. In the scene, both Andy's room and the spare room face the street instead of Opie's room as is normally seen.

In the fifth season episode "Family Visit," when Aunt Bee's baby sister Nora and her family come to visit, there again is

"It's yer shocks. Yer shocks."

no spare room. Instead of Nora and Ollie staying in a spare room, Ollie has to sleep with Andy. The next morning, Aunt Bee asks Andy how he slept. Referring to Uncle Ollie, he answers, "Well, half the night he had his arm in my mouth. The other half he was dreamin' he was ridin' a bicycle. All in all, I'd say it's one of the most active nights I ever spent." When Ollie comes into the kitchen, Aunt Bee says she heard he slept well, but he instead says, "Not a wink. Not a wink!"

At the end of the same season, a spare room reappears and is again actually seen when Andy begrudgingly helps Aunt Bee ready the room for his "cousin" Gloria who is coming to visit following a broken engagement.

Interestingly, while the existence of a spare room during the black and white seasons varied as dictated by the needs of the stories, a spare room is always shown to be available during the three color seasons. The Taylors prepare the room especially for Barney by adding a nightlight in "The Return of Barney Fife," and, of course, Barney stays in the spare room during later visits back to Mayberry. During the final season, Aunt Bee's cousin, Bradford, stays with the family, presumably in the spare room.

Bringing an extra chair into the spare bedroom in preparation for "cousin" Gloria's visit.

When it was seen, the spare room was always shown to be furnished. The single variation in this norm was used for comic effect in the seventh season episode, "Mind Over Matter." Goober believes his back has been seriously hurt in a slight fender bender after listening to Floyd describe a man who died after a similar back injury and after hearing Aunt Bee tell a similar story. Aunt Bee insists he come home with her since no one would be available to take care of him at his own place. Andy is surprised to find that Goober is recuperating in his bed. Aunt Bee tells Andy the situation is an emergency and Andy can "take the cot in the spare room."

When was the Taylor bathroom first seen?

In the 1960s, bathrooms were not typically shown with the thought being that it might shock the sensibilities of the public. Just a few years earlier, when the live version of *No Time for Sergeants* starring Andy Griffith was broadcast as an episode of *The United States Steel Hour* anthology series, the gag of toilet seats being rigged to "salute" in the latrine was vetoed by the network. And of course, just where a bathroom in the courthouse is located never shown.

So it is not surprising that the Taylor's bathroom is not typically seen. However, there are two exceptions. It is first seen in "Wedding Bells for Aunt Bee," originally broadcast April 2, 1962, near the end of the second season. While Aunt Bee and cleaner Fred Goss are at the movies, Opie fakes brushing his teeth by simply wetting his brush in an attempt to fool Andy.

Andy tells Opie the story of a little boy who used to wet his toothbrush to fool his dad and thought it was "a right funny joke" but eventually never smiled since he didn't have any teeth. Opie then went back into the bathroom to really brush them.

Just as in other shows of that era, when bathrooms were shown, they generally were not shown in full. So while a sink and mirror are seen, there is no sign of a shocking toilet.

Two seasons later, the bathroom is seen again, this time when house guest Gomer makes an inordinate amount of noise, first gargling and then loudly singing "No-Account Mule" while combing his hair in "Gomer the House Guest."

While not an important point for consistency, when the bathroom is first shown it is at the end of a hallway just after turning left when leaving Opie's room. The wall opposite the mirror in the bathroom is where the door is located. The next time the bathroom is seen, a window is on the wall opposite the mirror instead of a door.

By the next decade, the sound of Archie Bunker flushing the toilet was often heard, but the word remained taboo in Mayberry at least in reference to a commode. However, the word as part of the name "toilet water," an old-fashioned name for perfume, or technically, Eau de Toilette, is spoken by Aunt Bee when describing the perfume she wants at the drug store when Ellie Walker first came to Mayberry.

When did Barney first get locked in a cell?

The recurring gag of Barney accidentally locking himself in one of the jail cells appeared early in the series and continued for all five years Don Knotts was a regular in the show.

The gag is first seen in "Mayberry Goes Hollywood," originally aired on January 2, 1961. Andy and Barney are straightening one of the cells in anticipation of movie producer Mr. Harmon stopping by. While dusting, Barney pulls the cell door closed. When Andy realizes what Barney has done, it is clear that it is not the first time it has happened as Andy asks, "Barney! Again?" Andy uses the handle of a broom to try to get the keys which are in the other cell door. Just as it looks as though he will be successful, Barney sneezes and bumps into Andy, causing the keys to fall as Mr. Harmon enters the courthouse. After Harmon releases them from the cell and he and Andy leave for Andy to give him a tour of the town, Barney absentmindedly pulls the cell door shut after re-entering the cell, locking himself in again. During the epilogue of the episode, Andy and Opie enter the courthouse to find Barney has once again accidentally locked himself in the cell and is using the broom handle to try to get the keys just as Andy did.

The writers knew a good gag when they saw one. Barney was locked in a cell two more times before the first season was over. In "The New Doctor," when Andy leaves the courthouse under the mistaken notion that Ellie and the new doctor in town plan to marry, a frantic Barney is concerned there could be bloodshed and scrambles to retrieve his holster and gun in the cell. As he flings the door open, it bounces back shut behind him, locking him in once again. Just two episodes later in "The Inspector," Barney is nervous about a by-the-book representative from the State Inspector's Office. He sends Opie to the courthouse to bring Andy a hat and tie so he can be in full uniform, but Opie shows up with a fisherman's cap covered with lures and a polka dot tie. After Opie leaves, Andy puts them on to tease Barney which causes Barney to become even more worried. As Andy goes into the cell to place a pillow on the cot, Barney once again flings the cell door open causing it to bounce shut and lock behind them.

Likely realizing this was a gag that needed to be used more sparingly or it would get old, Barney still locked himself and sometimes Andy in a cell occasionally but the gag was used only once per season afterward.

In the second season episode "Sheriff Barney," officials in the town of Greendale decide to offer Barney the position of sheriff in their community based on an article in the *Mayberry Gazette* about Mayberry's low crime rate in which Andy praised his deputy for his help. As the men look at Barney's photo in the paper, one of them says he hopes Barney will be their next sheriff. He adds, "Barney Fife! So keen, alert, sharp!" The next scene opens with Barney walking into a cell carrying a blanket and once again flinging the door open hard enough that it bounces back and locks on its own. While the gag had not been used yet that season, Andy notes it was the third time that week Barney had done so. Andy must have taken pleasure in teasing Barney about this habit. When Andy opens the door, Barney mentions that he thought Andy was going to keep him locked in for a while like he always did.

During the third season, in "One Punch Opie" a new kid in town is leading Opie's friends astray. Andy has Opie bring his friends to the courthouse, though the new troublemaker refuses to come. Andy warns them about what will happen if they continue to misbehave. Rather than let the boys then leave, Barney insists on talking to them himself. Barney tells the children, "A man confined to prison is a man who has given up his liberty…his pursuit of happiness. No more carefree hours. No more doin' whatever ya' want whenever ya' want. No more peanut butter and jelly sandwiches." As he walks into the cell, he adds, "Take a good look, boys, because it definitely is no fun when that iron door clangs shut on you." To demonstrate the point, he pulls the door shut and then realizes what he had done.

Barney is locked in the cell again in the epilogue when he asks Leon, the small child who sometimes wanders through town silently offering people a bite of his peanut butter and jelly sandwich, to close the door. Barney meant the courthouse door, but little Leon misunderstands and closes the cell door.

The gag is again used during the fourth season in the epilogue of "Ernest T. Bass Joins the Army." Throughout the episode, Ernest T. keeps escaping from the cell to Andy and Barney's bewilderment. After Andy resolved the situation with the rock-throwing mountain man and Ernest T. returned to the hills, Barney searches the cell and finds a bent fork that he is sure must have been what Ernest T. used to escape. He has Andy come into the cell to show him the fork, then intentionally shuts the door to lock it and demonstrate how the fork could be used to open the door. Of course, it does not work and the keys are across the room in the filing cabinet.

The gag was used one more time during Don Knotts' final season playing the deputy in "Barney's Bloodhound." Barney believes he has trained a dog, Blue, to be an expert tracker although the dog obviously has no special abilities other than to leap on whoever blows a silent dog whistle. After the criminal Ralph Neal is captured and is being held in one of the cells, Andy is cleaning the other cell. Still trying to convince Andy of Blue's abilities, Barney holds the ring of cell keys under Blue's nose, telling the dog to sniff them. He then tosses the keys on the ground, telling Blue, "Go get it, boy!" The dog does not comply so Barney tries a second time and is thrilled when Blue picks up the ring of keys in his mouth. Barney then excitedly says all he needs to do now is teach Blue to fetch. He then urges the dog to bring him the keys though Blue sits still. Barney goes into the cell with Andy and, without thinking, closes the cell door. For a few moments, it looks like Blue might take the keys to Neal who also begins calling to the dog, but Andy has Barney blow the dog whistle which enables them to retrieve the keys.

"I tell you what we'll do in your case, though. If you're good--if you're very good--we'll throw some peanuts in your cell. You can jump up and down on them and make your own peanut butter."

When were the "Fun Girls" first seen?

Just like the larger-than-life Ernest T. Bass, the two "Fun Girls from Mount Pilot" were also used sparingly.

The duo made up of Skippy and Daphne debuted in the third season's "Barney Mends a Broken Heart," first aired November 5, 1962. The two women are archetypes of the "dumb blonde" with abrasive personalities. Skippy was reportedly so named as an homage to Skippy Pyle, Denver Pyle's older sister who was Sheldon Leonard's valued assistant. In the episode, Andy has a spat with nurse Peggy over an old college friend of hers named Don. As an inside joke used as a nod to Don Knotts, when Andy speaks to Barney, he asks, "Guess what his name was?" When Barney shakes his head that he doesn't know, Andy says, "Don. Wouldn't 'cha know his name would be Don?" After his attempt to fix Andy up with the morose Lydia Crosswaithe is unsuccessful, Barney calls Skippy, a woman he met at the Tip Top Cafe a few weeks earlier in Mount Pilot. He arranges for her to bring her friend, Daphne, whom he had also met, and meet at the cafe. Barney then convinces Andy to go by telling him he has received an anonymous tip that the cafe was selling liquor. The implication is that Mount Pilot is in Mayberry County since Andy would have no jurisdiction in a neighboring county. Yet the previous season, Andy spoke to Sheriff Mitchell in Mount Pilot, meaning it was in a different county. The small inconsistency is another of those fun facts to note that in no way diminishes the value of the storytelling.

When the "fun girls" come into the cafe and Andy realizes what Barney has done, he has no choice but to allow them to sit in the booth with them. The deep-voiced Daphne immediately rubs her shoulder up against Andy's shoulder. Skippy has a distinctive braying laugh and perennially calls Barney "Bernie" despite his repeated corrections. The women often argue with one another, talking over one another as they do so. After Andy apologizes for the misunderstanding, a large man Daphne apparently sees at times named Al comes into the cafe and spots them. After a short argument, Al grabs Barney to punch him. Andy intervenes which results in his getting a black eye.

Skippy and Daphne were seen for less than four minutes in "Barney Mends a Broken Heart," but their strong characters made a lasting impression. The episode is the first of seven episodes of *The Andy Griffith Show* written by producer and story consultant Aaron Ruben. Skippy and Daphne return for an episode near the end of the following season also written by Ruben with a title that gave them the name by which they are usually called: "Fun Girls."

While Andy and Barney are working late doing inventory with plans to see Helen and Thelma Lou afterward, Barney goes out to get food they can eat in the courthouse while they are working. When Barney comes back late and empty-handed, he explains he has run into some old friends who insisted on paying them a visit. Skippy and Daphne then burst in, with Skippy yelling, "Surprise!" Daphne walks up to Andy, rubs her shoulder against his just as she had done the last time, and says in her distinctive, deep voice, "Hello, doll." Skippy not only continues to call Barney "Bernie," she now also frequently pushes the deputy by the shoulder causing him to veer off balance. While Barney is showing Skippy one cell, Daphne gets Andy inside the other cell, slams the door shut, and sings in a sing-song voice, "I'm locked up with the sheriff!" As Barney struggles to unlock the door while Skippy tries to tug him into the other cell, Daphne keeps Andy in a bear hug and says, "Oh, sheriff, come on. Let's play big house!" The women again argue with one another, this time over whose friend Al was between them. In order to try to end the situation, Andy and Barney agree to drive them back to Mount Pilot but are spotted by Helen and Thelma Lou while doing so. The next day, Helen and Thelma Lou break their dates to go to a dance with the lawmen. Thelma Lou adds, "Shouldn't be hard for you to get yourselves another date. Why don't you take the two young ladies who were with you last night when you were…working? They looked like fun girls!"

That night, Barney still shows up at Andy's house to pick him up for the dance and explains they would not be going stag. He snaps his fingers and the "fun girls" come in, giggling loudly with Skippy again yelling, "Surprise!" When a shocked Aunt Bee is followed out of the kitchen by Opie, Daphne kneels down and asks Opie if he is going to be a sheriff when he grows up. Skippy says, "Oh, no, Daph. You know how that works. The son of a cop is usually a gangster."

This is the same episode that introduces the character of Goober, which is undoubtedly one of the reasons Ruben chose to also write the episode since Gomer was about to leave for his own spin-off series which Ruben had created. When the lawmen and the fun girls arrive at the dance, they see Helen and Thelma

Lou are there with Gomer and Goober. After Andy and Barney convince Helen and Thelma Lou it had all been a misunderstanding, as they are leaving they see Skippy and Daphne squealing with laughter at the table with Gomer and Goober, clearly delighted with Goober's impressions.

The "fun girls" appear one last time. Near the end of the fifth season, "The Arrest of the Fun Girls" aired. Unlike the previous two, the episode was written by Richard Powell, the last of four episodes he wrote for the series.

Andy and Barney are in the courthouse when they hear a car horn blaring and the screech of tires. They run outside and see a convertible speeding down the road then get in the squad car and give pursuit. When they stop the car, they discover it is being driven by Daphne with Skippy in the passenger seat. The "fun girls" have been speeding intentionally so they would be stopped by Andy and Barney. When Andy explains they were doing 45 MPH on a street with a 20 MPH speed limit, Skippy says, "Yeah, take us to jail!" then laughs. Andy and Barney drive the the duo to the county line and promise they will look them up the next time they are in Mount Pilot and give them a ticket then. Thankful Helen and Thelma Lou had not seen Skippy and Daphne, they return to town.

Apparently, Andy or Barney had also told the duo they had to work in the courthouse that night. As they are leaving to meet Helen and Thelma Lou, the "fun girls" come in, with Skippy yelling, as usual, "Surprise!" They say they felt sorry that Andy and Barney had to work that night so they brought a picnic dinner to eat in the courthouse and a radio to provide music for dancing. The women again want to "play jail" so Andy decides to leave them in the cells with Barney watching them with the lights out while he goes to take Helen and Thelma Lou for something to eat and then home, making an excuse why Barney couldn't be there. Skippy and Daphne do fall asleep in the cell but are awakened when an intoxicated Otis comes into the courthouse and is upset that his cell is "filled with women." At the same time, Helen and Thelma Lou insist on riding by the courthouse in case Barney is awake and would like a sandwich and some company. Inside the courthouse, after Barney has sent Otis home, Skippy wants to dance and whenever Barney turns the lights off, she flips them back on, leading to Helen and Thelma Lou learning the "fun girls" were in the courthouse. After Helen and Thelma Lou leave, Andy finally loses his temper and makes Skippy and Daphne leave as well. He then says to Barney, "Well, it's been quite a night. So far we've lost four girls and one drunk."

After Helen and Thelma Lou once again forgive them, Barney says to Andy he has been thinking about the nightmare they have been through and concluded, "Our only crime is that we're attractive to women." After picking their girlfriends up for a quiet dinner prepared by Aunt Bee, the situation goes wrong once more when they discover the "fun girls" have shown up at Andy's house. Helen and Thelma Lou are again upset and leave. Barney suggests to Andy's disbelief that they make the best of the situation since it is Saturday night and the duo from Mount Pilot are good dancers.

In the epilogue, Andy and Barney are sitting on the bench in front of the courthouse when a car speeds past them down Main Street. The concerned Barney first says the car must have been doing 50 and, when asked, describes the car as an old jalopy with two women in it. Realizing it is the "fun girls" again, Andy says, "Actually, I didn't think they 'as doing 50. Maybe 40." Barney says he would guess 30 and Andy says actually closer to 25 or 20.

What was a business
first seen in Mayberry?

The first business seen in Mayberry was shown in the opening scene of the pilot episode "Danny Meets Andy Griffith" on *The Danny Thomas Show*, first broadcast February 15, 1960. As the cars pull up in front of the courthouse and Danny Williams exits his car, a hardware store is briefly visible with a sign that reads "Amos Jacobs Hardware." The name of the hardware store is an inside joke. Danny Thomas was born to immigrant parents from Lebanon and his actual birth name was Amos Muzyad Yahkoob Kairouz. When Danny began performing, he eventually used an Anglicized version of his name: Amos Jacobs. Hence the name on the hardware store. Of course, he later changed his name to Danny Thomas, taking the name from two of his brothers, Daniel and Thomas. By the way, since *The Danny Thomas Show* was filmed in a studio before an audience, both Danny's car and the squad car are missing their windows to prevent reflections and glare. It is also worth noting that, while the barbershop is not the first business seen in the pilot, it is in the same location by the courthouse in the pilot as it later is in the spin-off.

In interior courthouse shots during the first season of *The Andy Griffith Show*, what appears to be a builder's business is across the street from the courthouse though in exterior shots no such business exists. The sign painted on the backdrop is not clearly visible but can be seen if one looks closely in "The New Housekeeper," which first aired October 3, 1960. The business sign can be first seen through the courthouse window as Barney is preparing to fingerprint Emma Brand for jaywalking. The partially visible sign can be seen to include the letters "_WZK BUIL__ERS." The business is seen throughout the first season as the producers, at first not knowing if the show was going to last, simply used a generic backdrop to represent businesses on a town street. By the second season, a backdrop that accurately reflected the buildings seen in exterior shots filmed on the Forty Acres Backlot was used.

The backdrop seen through the window in the upper left of the photo does not match what was across the street on the backlot where exteriors were filmed.

The first business to be seen clearly in *The Andy Griffith Show* that remained a fixture was seen in the second episode, "Manhunt," originally aired on October 10, 1960. While it does not play a role in that episode's storyline, the business is the town's barbershop, which can only be described as appropriate considering the town center it is eventually shown to be. (The movie theater was technically seen first but in a pan shot that was fading in after the previous shot which resulted in it not being seen clearly.) The barbershop has a large sign that reads "Barber Shop" (using the older-fashion spelling as two words) mounted on the wall above the awning, a sign that disappears after just two more episodes. While it is not seen clearly in "Manhunt," as Andy walks down the sidewalk to where Jim Lindsey is playing in the following episode, "The Guitar Player," the barbershop is shown to take up the windows on both sides of the doorway in the alcove. (It later took up only the space between the alcove and the courthouse.) The signs read only "Barber Shop" with no reference to Floyd, the character having not been introduced as the barber at this point. In fact, the window of the barbershop lists the barber's name in small lettering as Sid Elson.

While the barber's name of Sid Elson is not easy to see, it is visible in multiple shots in early episodes.

The first Mayberry business seen in the series that actually figured into the storyline is also in "The Guitar Player" when Orville Monroe is upset that Jim Lindsey is playing guitar in front of Orville's funeral parlor. As Jim plays in front of the window which reads "Funeral Parlor and Mortuary," Orville demands Andy arrest Lindsey for disturbing the peace. Andy says, "Well now, Orville, let's be realistic about that thing. In your business, I don't rightly see who he could be disturbin.'"

When was the license plate on the Mayberry squad car first seen clearly?

The squad car was not seen in full in the first episode when Aunt Bee came to live with Andy and Opie. Only part of it was seen as Andy was waxing the car. In the second episode, "Manhunt," first broadcast on October 10, 1960, when Barney comes to the lake where Andy and Opie have been fishing to tell them the big—really big—news that the State Police are coming, the license plate is seen in full. The plate number is the familiar JL-327 which was seen for the bulk of the series.

JL-327, the license plate usually seen on the squad car.

However, the next time the Mayberry squad car is seen the license plate has changed. In the fourth episode of the series, "Ellie Comes to Town,"

DC-269 was first seen in "Ellie Comes to Town."

when Barney drops Andy and Aunt Bee off at Walker's Drugstore and they are surprised it is closed, the squad car plate is now DC-269. That plate number had actually been seen before. Two episodes earlier in "Manhunt," the same episode when the regular Mayberry squad car plates were first clearly seen, the DC-269 plate was on the lead car in the procession of State Police vehicles when they arrived in front of the courthouse.

The Mayberry squad car plate is next seen two episodes later in "Runaway Kid" though only fleetingly. When Opie and his friends push the squad car in front of a fire hydrant, just as one camera shot dissolves into another, the plate can be seen to have returned back to JL-327. But in the next three episodes, "Andy the Matchmaker" "Opie's Charity," and "A Feud Is a Feud," the plate switches again to DC-269.

The squad car plate is not seen again until Episode 11, "Christmas Story" at which point it returns permanently to the original JL-327, staying the same the rest of the series.

It is interesting to note that while the plate appears to the audience to switch back and forth several times with no explanation, it actually did so only once. To viewers, it appears the plate changes to DC-269 for the single episode of "Ellie Comes to Town" then changes back to JL-327 in "Runaway Kid" then back to DC-269 again for several episodes beginning with "Andy the Matchmaker". This appearance is actually the result of "Ellie Comes to Town" being shown in a different order than it had been filmed. While it aired as the fourth episode, it was actually the sixth episode filmed.

Once the plates returned permanently to the original JL-327 in "Christmas Story," it did not mean the DC-269 plates were never to be seen again. During the first half of Season 2, the DC-269 license plates were seen on State Attorney Bob Roger's car, on "handyman" Henry Wheeler's

DC-269 appears again in "Barney's Replacement."

truck, on The Esquire Club member Roger Courtney's convertible, and on Joe Water's illegally parked car.

Both DC-269 and JL-327 license plates could be seen hanging as part of a collection of license plates in the front room of Goober's garage in the second season of *Mayberry R.F.D.!*

An alert Mayberry fan, Jack Fellenzer, discovered the likely reason JL-327 was chosen as the license plate number for the Mayberry squad car. A series of magazine print ads for Atlas Tires ran shortly before the series began that featured license plates from the United States and Canadian provinces. Presumably, the plate numbers used in the ads would have been verified to not be actual plate numbers. The North Carolina plate shown in the ads was JL-327 which was then appropriated to serve as the squad car's license plate number.

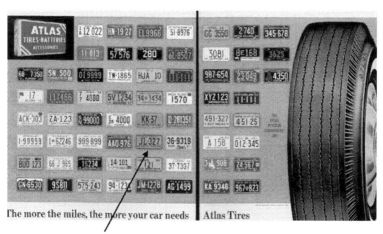

When was the first
ordinance number stated?

Ordinances, or local laws, governing Mayberry were often cited by code number, usually by the overly officious Barney.

Laws were sometimes referred to without providing a section number. For example, in "Black Day for Mayberry" in Season 4, when trying to get townspeople who had come to see the gold truck to disperse, Andy simply tells them they will be interfering with government property if they don't leave.

When numbers were given, it is nearly always for comic effect. While arrests had been made in earlier episodes, the first time a specific code number is heard is nearly two-thirds of the way through the first season in "Andy Saves Barney's Morale" on February 20, 1961. While Andy is away in Centerville having left Barney as Acting Sheriff, Barney arrests enough people to have both cells packed tight. Jud Fletcher's is the first case heard when Andy returned. Barney says in a clipped tone that Jud is charged with a violation of municipal code number 721-8, disturbing the peace. Andy is incredulous that Jud is charged with that violation. Jud says, "I ain't had the strength to disturb the peace nigh on to 30 years!" The comedy continues when Andy has Jud yell, "Chester Jones, you're a two-faced cheatin' liar" at the top of his lungs which, of course, was a quite feeble "yell." This is followed by Aunt Bee having been charged with a violation of code number 421, unlawful assemblage and inciting a riot (which would actually be two different crimes and would not be under the same code number). By the time Barney gets to Mayor Pike's charge of having violated code number 439, vagrancy and loitering (again, properly two separate charges), Barney is too embarrassed to even read the ordinance number and charge aloud.

The show was inconsistent in numbering. While disturbing the peace is a violation of 721-8 with Jud, it is a 302 when Naylor and Maudie are brought in for fighting in "Andy's Vacation." (They are also charged with a 710: Assault with a deadly weapon. In this case, the weapon was a live chicken.) In Season 2, loitering is instead a violation of code number 63 when hobo Dave Browne is brought in (though vagrancy would have seemed the more logical charge) instead of a 439 as it had been for Mayor Pike. Parking near a fire hydrant is a violation of "Rule" 8, Section B when Barney checks "Quiet Sam" Becker's truck but is a 115 in "Aunt Bee's Medicine Man." But the winner has to be public intoxication or drunkenness. It is a 404-B, a 411, and a 502.

While Barney is fond of citing specific codes, Andy often is not. When Barney brings in Naylor and Maudie for fighting as mentioned above, Andy says, "Barney, I'm too tired to look up the numbers. What were they doin'?"

Two additional good examples of the numbers being used for comic effect are found in "The Darlings Are Coming." When Andy is called to the Mayberry Hotel by John Masters who suspects there are more people in the single-occupancy room than just Briscoe Darling, Andy tells John he knows who they are and had warned them earlier on a 907. Without missing a beat, John immediately knows a 907 meant dipping a hat in the horse trough. Later, after the Darlings have left the hotel and are found trespassing in an empty store, Briscoe asks Andy, "What number did we commit now?" (By the way, it was a 317: occupancy of private property without permission of the owner.)

When was Goober's last name revealed to be Pyle?

Mayberry fans take the position that Goober's last name was Pyle from the beginning. Books about *The Andy Griffith Show* and other sources consistently state that Goober's last name was "Pyle." These are clearly correct in retrospect. However, when the character was first seen by the viewing audience, his last name was not actually stated to be Pyle. This situation did not change for quite some time.

In early references to the character before the part had been cast, Gomer specifically stated that Goober was his cousin. Of course, that would not necessarily mean they had the same last name. No last name is provided when Goober is first seen in "Fun Girls" on April 3, 1964. In this and subsequent episodes, the character is always listed in the show credits, the scripts, and public releases of information such as *TV Guide* listings simply as Goober.

The first time a reference is made to his last name is nearly a year later in "TV or Not TV," first aired on March 1, 1965, when Andy introduces him as Goober Beasley. In this particular script, the dialogue does state this as his full name. However, in subsequent scripts and in the credits, the character continued to be referred to as simply Goober. By the end of the fifth season, his name still has not been clearly stated to be Pyle.

Even though Goober was introduced in the fourth season, the full name of the character was not established as Goober Pyle until the sixth season of *The Andy Griffith Show*, and even then it occurred in a different show! Goober's last name is stated to be Pyle for the first time in a crossover episode of the spin-off *Gomer Pyle-USMC* which aired well over a year and a half after Goober was first seen in *The Andy Griffith Show*. In the episode "A Visit from Cousin Goober" which first aired on November 26, 1965, Goober causes much confusion in Camp Henderson when he walks onto the base while the sentry is looking the other way. (That seems to happen disturbingly often at the military base.) Even though Gomer tells Goober he has to leave the base and arranges to meet him in town, Goober goes back into the barracks while Sergeant Carter leads Gomer and the others on a hike. He tries on one of Gomer's uniforms and is discovered by superior officers while wearing the uniform but slouching with his hands in his pockets and still wearing his two-tone shoes. Thinking he is a Marine who has been confined to barracks, the officer asks him his name. Goober replies, "Pyle. What's yours?"

It was late in the same season before Goober's last name of Pyle is first used in *The Andy Griffith Show*. In "The Battle of Mayberry," first broadcast on April 4, 1966, Opie has to write a paper for school about the local historic battle. After Floyd tells Opie his ancestor, Colonel Caleb "Stonewall" Lawson was the hero of the battle, Goober expresses disbelief. He explains, "Well, it just so happens one of my kinfolk was the hero—Colonel Goober Pyle of the North Carolina Seventh Cavalry. I never even heard of no Colonel Lawson." While Goober does not specifically state his last name is Pyle, the episode confirmed what by that point had already been firmly established in his appearance in *Gomer Pyle-USMC*.

When was Goober's distinctive cap first seen?

When George Lindsey as Goober took over the archetype previously played so well by Jim Nabors as Gomer, he decided from the beginning he would do everything he could to make the character different and his own.

When Goober is first actually seen in "The Fun Girls," he does wear a hat though not the one that became his trademark. By the way, many fans are often surprised that Goober's introductory episode was the only time the two characters ever appeared together in *The Andy Griffith Show*, though of course, they did appear together once in the spin-off *Gomer Pyle-USMC* and in the reunion movie *Return to Mayberry*.

Goober is not seen again until nearly a third of the way through the next season. On November 23, 1964, in "Goodbye Sheriff Taylor," Barney is left in charge while Andy is considering a move to Raleigh. Goober is brought in as a potential deputy. The mechanic is wearing the hat which quickly became associated with him.

The whoopee cap with no holes.

The technical name for such a hat is a whoopee cap. It is made by taking a brimmed felt hat and removing the brim. The bottom edge of the crown is cut in a zig-zag pattern and folded up to form a band. Whoopee caps were a fad particularly with young people during the mid-20th century and were usually decorated with buttons.

A whoopee cap is similar to a beanie, which is a cap made from triangles of fabric with a button on top (though a brief fad was to top them with propellers) and no band around the bottom. As a result of their similar shape, the type of cap Goober wore is quite often called a beanie by Mayberry fans.

A whoopee cap had actually been seen earlier in the series. In the third season episode "One-Punch Opie," Billy Gray wears one. Billy is one of Opie's friends who falls under the bad influence of Steve Quincy, a new boy in town.

The whoopee cap with holes.

George Lindsey said growing up he saw mechanics sometimes wear these caps to protect their eyes from anything that might drip on their heads while working on cars. Since Goober had taken over Gomer's position at Wally's Filling Station after Gomer enlisted, he thought a whoopee cap would be appropriate and, of course, would be different from the ball cap Gomer always wore while on the job. After the first time he wore the cap, Lindsey had the idea of cutting holes in the cap as he had observed mechanics sometimes did so to allow for ventilation. Holes were added for the cap's second appearance three episodes later. Lindsey also wore a pocket protector with pens and tire gauges as another distinguishing point from Gomer. He always kept the pocket items in the same order.

When was Howard Sprague first seen?

After Gomer Pyle and Barney Fife were no longer regular characters in Mayberry, the producers relied on Goober and Floyd to pick up some of the comedic slack, along with using Aunt Bee and her friend, Clara, more often. The attempt to introduce a new deputy to take Barney's place was far from a success, so the producers were open to introducing new comedic characters.

Jack Dodson co-starred with Jason Robards in Eugene O'Neill's short play, *Hughie*, a two-man Broadway show. The production later toured nationally which included a stint in Los Angeles. Andy Griffith and his wife saw the West Coast production. Griffith went backstage to introduce himself to the actors and complimented Dodson on his performance. Deciding to stay in Los Angeles to seek work, Dodson hoped Griffith's complimentary attitude might lead to him joining the cast of *The Andy Griffith Show*.

Unfortunately, when Dodson's agent arranged for him to meet with Mike Fenton, the casting director for *The Andy Griffith Show,* it went nowhere. Afterward, Dodson's agent called Fenton to tell him the story of Andy coming backstage after seeing *Hughie*. When Fenton then contacted Griffith saying Dodson had indicated he had met Griffith but failing to mention it was after Griffith had seen Dodson in a play, the series' star said he had no idea who Dodson was. After both Fenton and Dodson's agent thought the actor might have fabricated the exchange, the casting director agreed to broach the subject with Griffith once more but the star still said he had absolutely no idea who Dodson was.

Not long after Dodson's unfruitful attempts to land an audition, Griffith and his wife saw a film together. Griffith was not impressed with the movie and as they were driving home, he told his wife the best acting he had seen recently was in the play that had starred only two men. Griffith then suddenly realized who Dodson  was. He immediately had someone contact Dodson and ask him to come to the Forty Acres Backlot where exteriors were filmed. Griffith apologized for the misunderstanding and had Dodson meet with Aaron Ruben. Dodson first appeared in *The Andy Griffith Show* two-thirds of the way through the sixth season as Ed Jenkins, the Taylor's disappointed insurance agent, in "Lost and Found." Seven episodes later, Dodson returned in "The County Clerk" playing the ongoing role for which he is best remembered: milquetoast and mama's boy Howard Sprague. The episode was first broadcast on March 14, 1966. Howard became a regular character on *The Andy Griffith Show* and then in the spin-off *Mayberry R.F.D.*

Dodson credited Ruben with coming up with much of Howard's character, but credit also must go to one of the writers of "The County Clerk." The episode was written by frequent Mayberry writers Bill Idelson and Sam Bobrick. Idelson not only wrote; he also acted. He played Herman Glimscher, a similar, milquetoast character still tied to his mother's apron strings who was the sometime boyfriend of Sally Rogers in *The Dick Van Dyke Show*.

When was Millie Hutchins first seen?

As Jack Dodson developed the character of Howard Sprague, he became concerned that the joke of being under his mother's thumb was initially funny but eventually would grow old. He recalled thinking that the character would gradually become more pathetic than amusing and so approached Andy Griffith about making a change in Howard's circumstances by having the character of Howard's mother leave the show. Howard's manipulative mother was played by Mabel Albertson, the sister of actor Jack Albertson. She was a busy character actress and was not under contract to *The Andy Griffith Show*, so the suggested change was incorporated into the show.

As an additional way to broaden the character, a potential girlfriend was introduced for Howard during the final season. Millie Hutchins was first seen in "Howard's Main Event," originally aired October 16, 1967. Played by Arlene Golonka who had played Candy Starr on Broadway in *One Flew Over the Cuckoo's Nest*, Millie is a new employee at Boysinger Bakery. In her debut episode, Howard has to stand up to a bully in order to spend time with her. Six episodes later, they have been seeing one another "every night for the past month now. Uh, that is, except for the nights she had to wash her hair." Howard proposes and Millie happily accepts, and they plan to get married right away in Wheeling where her parents live. However, on the train trip to West Virginia, they mutually realize they are rushing marriage and call off the wedding.

Even though Millie appears only twice in *The Andy Griffith Show*, she stayed in Mayberry as a regular character in *Mayberry R.F.D.* Millie became the love interest of the spin-off series' lead character Sam Jones. For some reason, she is then known as Millie Swanson though she is clearly the same character who had appeared twice in *The Andy Griffith Show*. She still works at Boysinger Bakery and it is made clear that she and Howard used to see one another. In the second episode of the spin-off, "The Harvest Ball," when discussing whom Goober is likely to ask to the dance, Howard says he is sure it would be Millie Swanson. Emmett asks whether Howard used to go with Millie. Howard responds, "Yeah. We were quite an item, as they say in the columns, but, uh… Well, we decided it would never work out on a long term basis."

When was Emmett Clark first seen?

The health of Howard McNear deteriorated during the seventh season of *The Andy Griffith Show*, so much so that the wonderful actor would become frustrated and upset when he could not remember his lines. McNear left the show at the end of the season. His absence at the beginning of the eighth and final season was filled by a new character, Emmett Clark. The owner of a fix-it shop, Emmett took over the space that had previously held the barbershop.

Emmett was mentioned before he was seen. In the eighth season opener, "Opie's First Love," Opie and Arnold come into the courthouse asking for help with Arnold's broken record player. Goober says that Emmett Clark fixes radios and Andy tells the boys he will take it to see if it can be fixed. Emmett was first seen in the next episode "Howard the Bowler" which originally aired on September 18, 1967. Andy mentions

to Opie that Emmett provided bowling shirts for free to the Mayberry bowling team since he is a new businessman and the shirts acted as advertising, explaining, "Some of those bowling matches... I guess 50, 60 people get to see that name." An impressed Opie can only utter the word, "Wow!"

Emmett was played by Paul Hartman who meshed with the cast and quickly fit in as an ongoing character. Hartman began his career as a ballroom dancer and upon occasion later showed off his dancing skills in *Mayberry R.F.D.* After Hartman and his wife, Grace, both won Tony Awards for their performances in the Broadway revue *Angels in the Wings*, they starred in one of the earliest television sitcoms, *The Hartmans,* in 1949 though the series lasted only two months. He appeared in more than half of the episodes of the final season of *The Andy Griffith Show* and became a series regular in *Mayberry R.F.D.*

The fix-it shop owner's name was an homage to Emmett Forrest, a childhood and lifelong friend of Griffith's who still resided in Griffith's hometown, Mount Airy, North Carolina. Over the years, Griffith gave many props and artifacts from the show to Forrest who preserved them. Over the years, some of the items were displayed in a Mount Airy visitor's center and then in a section of a local shop. But in 2009, a beautiful new building was dedicated to house the largest collection of artifacts in existence about Andy Griffith's career in theater, film, and music. Griffith, his wife, and various members of the cast and crew donated many items. However, an enormous portion of the rare items was donated by Forrest who was named the founding curator of The Andy Griffith Museum. A substantial and extensive renovation of the museum in 2017 transformed the already-fine museum into a state-of-the-art experience.

When was Sam Jones first seen?

While the quality of *The Andy Griffith Show* may not have been as high during the last three years of color episodes compared to the first five black and white seasons, the show remained immensely popular with the public. Mayberry provided a comforting and familiar refuge from the civil strife of the 1960s in "the real world." The show had proved it could survive the loss of Don Knotts as Barney Fife by remaining in the top 10 in the Nielsen's after his departure. In fact, the eighth and final season of *The Andy Griffith Show* saw it reach the number one spot for the first and only time.

General Foods, the show's sponsor, and the CBS network executives understandably did not want the popular show to end. The decision was made to re-tool the show into what was technically a spin-off but really was closer to a continuation or reboot of the same show with a new title.

Bob Ross, the producer of the color episodes, was tasked with creating the new show. In order to launch the new series, the character of Sam Jones was introduced in "Sam for Town Council," an episode of *The Andy Griffith Show* first aired on March 11, 1968.

Farmer and newly-elected councilman Sam Jones was portrayed by Ken Berry, a talented actor who was also a song-and-dance man. Like Paul Hartman, Berry was able upon occasion to later show off his dancing skills in *Mayberry R.F.D.* While Berry had previously played recurring roles in the TV series *Dr. Kildare* and *Ensign O'Toole*, he first became widely known as Captain Wilton Parmenter on *F Troop* which ran from 1965 to 1967. He came to *Mayberry R.F.D.* fresh from the comedy Western.

Sam filled the same role Andy Griffith had as Andy Taylor. He was the straight man surrounded by a cast of colorful characters. Just like Andy, Sam was a widower raising a young son and in a position of some authority as the newly-elected head of Mayberry's town council. Sam appeared in the last four episodes of *The Andy Griffith Show*. The final episode was titled "Mayberry R.F.D.," the same title that was to be used for the spin-off series.

The original concept for the new show had been to put a somewhat different spin on the original show's premise. As seen in the pilot, Sam has arranged to have an old Army friend from Italy whom he has not seen in seven years move to America and work for him on his farm. Sam is taken aback when his old friend, Mario, arrives but is not alone. He has brought his elderly father and beautiful sister to live and work on the farm as well. However, when *Mayberry R.F.D.* premiered on September 23, 1968, the viewing public learned the decision had been made to scrap the inclusion of the Italian family and instead keep the spin-off as close as possible to its parent series. Aunt Bee remained in the cast as the new housekeeper for Sam and his son. Goober, Howard, and Emmett all also became series regulars with the spin-off remaining extremely popular. It ranked number four in the Nielsen ratings its first season.

The opening episode of *Mayberry R.F.D.* was the highest-rated episode of any series up to that point. In "Andy and Helen Get Married," the two finally become husband and wife with Opie in attendance and Barney having returned to serve as Andy's best man. Griffith then guest-starred as Sheriff Taylor in three additional episodes and was also sometimes referenced as still being in town even when not seen.   Behind the scenes, Griffith served as Executive Producer and came in periodically to provide input on the show's direction.

After Griffith's guest appearances, it became clear the sheriff and his family had moved away. Andy and Helen return a final time in the opening episode of the second season of *Mayberry R.F.D.* in "Andy's Baby," when they come back to Mayberry to have their new son Andy Jr. christened.

There were two other behind-the-scenes connections to the earlier series. First, Berry certainly won the role on his own, but he was a client of Dick Linke who was also Griffith's manager. Second, Berry was married to Jackie Joseph at the time. Joseph had appeared in Mayberry only once but was a popular character referred to several times in later episodes. In the classic episode "My Fair Ernest T. Bass," Joseph played Ramona Ancrum, or as the wild rock-throwing mountain man always called her, his "sweet Romeena."

Reprise: When was the town of Mayberry first referenced?

The third essay in this book addressed not only when the town name of Mayberry was first referenced in *The Andy Griffith Show* but also the origin of the name.

As the show developed, in many ways, the town became a character itself. Exterior shots of *The Andy Griffith Show* were filmed on the Forty Acres Backlot which at that time was owned by Desilu. The backlot had been the filming location for many movies and television shows. For example, Mayberry's old Remshaw "haunted house" was Aunt Pittypat's house in *Gone With the Wind*. Most scenes set at the lake in which a person actually entered the water, such as when Andy's boat sank with "jinx" Henry Bennett aboard, were filmed in a manmade lagoon on the backlot that had originally served as the filming location for the Johnny Weissmuller *Tarzan* films. After watching the Mayberry residents in the town for eight seasons, the Forty Acres Backlot became a real place to the series' loyal viewers, even though the "buildings" were actually nothing more than simple facades held up with scaffolding.

Like other shows at the time with a title including the name of a well-known lead actor such as *The Danny Thomas Show* and *The Dick Van Dyke Show*, the Mayberry series was named after Andy Griffith. The star later recalled that eventually, he and show creator Sheldon Leonard discussed that the show could have been titled after the town of Mayberry itself. Even acknowledging that the series was centered on Andy and Opie Taylor, the simple town and its eccentric residents were arguably a large part of the reason fans kept tuning in year after year in such high numbers.

When *The Andy Griffith Show* finally ended after eight seasons, it was decided the spin-off would indeed be named for the town. When *The Andy Griffith Show* went off the air, it was ranked number one in the Nielsen ratings, one of only three shows to hold this distinction. (The other two are *I Love Lucy* and *Seinfeld*.) The spin-off's name, *Mayberry R.F.D.*, implicitly acknowledged the concept that the town was, in essence, a character. *Mayberry R.F.D.* also proved to be a popular show, ranking number four in the Nielsens its first two seasons. The spin-off dropped to a still highly-ranked number fifteen its final season.

While there is no way to independently verify this, perhaps the drop in ratings was due to a change in the exterior filming location during the final season. While "Mayberry" was on the same Forty Acres Backlot all eight seasons of the original series and the first two of the spin-off, the production was moved to the Warner Brothers backlot during *Mayberry R.F.D.*'s third and final season. The changes were jarring after a decade of filming on the Forty Acres Backlot.

In the premier episode of *Mayberry R.F.D.*'s third season, "Emmett's Domestic Problem," originally aired on September 14, 1970, the first ongoing business seen is Emmett's Fix-It Shop. Instead of the familiar appearance of the shop in the same space that had always housed Floyd's Barber Shop for seven seasons in *The Andy Griffith Show,* Emmett's shop has a clearly different appearance. The brick color is not the same. The TV Repair shop that had been in the storefront on the other side of the shop is gone and instead a solid brick wall is in its place. The market is no longer down the street in its original location. Instead, it is around the corner from Emmett's shop and has a corner window.

Later episodes continued to show substantial changes. Goober's gas station is now in town with houses across the street. The producers tried to explain away some changes, such as stating in the third episode that Goober has opened a new gas station in town. But there is no explaining away major changes in Mayberry's appearance, such as Boysinger's Bakery now being across from a park in the town square which includes a gazebo. This new town of Mayberry could never be mistaken for the original.

There is no way to know without question whether this substantial and abrupt change in the appearance of the town of Mayberry affected the ratings, but the third season of *Mayberry R.F.D.* did see it fall out of the top 10, a first for any of the three Mayberry-related series. However, the drop in ratings were not the cause of the show's cancellation. Instead, the series ended as part of the notorious "rural purge" by CBS in which the majority of its rural-themed shows were canceled in 1971. Among other shows canceled at the same time were *The Beverly Hillbillies*, *Green Acres*, *Hee-Haw*, and *Lassie*. The original plan by CBS had been to renew *Mayberry R.F.D.* for the 1971-1972 season while canceling the other series, but the decision was ultimately made to end it along with the other rural-themed shows.

The final episode of *Mayberry R.F.D.* aired on March 29, 1971, spelling the end of Mayberry until the popular 1986 reunion made-for-television movie, *Return to Mayberry*.

Appendix

Unfortunately, the version of "The Darlings Are Coming" currently available on the Paramount DVD release and through the current streaming versions is heavily edited. Many fans do not realize they are not seeing the full version but it is obvious just by looking at the running time of "The Darlings Are Coming" compared to the running time of all the other episodes of the series.

There are five edits in the readily available versions.

First, in the scene by the horse trough, right after Charlene whistles at Andy, Briscoe explains to him, "Outside me and her brothers, they ain't no fellas left in the mountains for her to play with. You're mighty refreshin' to her."

The second scene edited is in the hotel room. After Charlene points out that Other, one of her brothers, is still outside, Briscoe says, "So he be. Don't have much personality, that boy." Briscoe then leans out of the window, throws down the rope, and shouts, "Here, Other. Climb aboard!"

On the currently available versions, the family is next shown playing an instrumental in the hotel room where Briscoe tells them when they finish they need to do better if they are going to play for Charlene and Dud's wedding. This is actually the end of the original scene. In the unedited version, as they first play, Charlene is initially standing by the mirror. As she walks toward Briscoe, Jebbin playfully kicks her and she returns a playful slap at his leg. She then sits down behind Briscoe, takes off his hat, and puts it on a table. Briscoe continues his jugging as he puts his hat back on.

The fourth edit is in the scene where the Darlings are staying in the Mayberry Jail. In the readily available versions, Briscoe is surprised Andy plays guitar, saying, "I didn't know you strang!" Andy joins them as they play an instrumental with Charlene continuing to flirt with Andy. Immediately after the song ends, the next scene shows the Darlings waiting at the bus stop.

In the unedited version, after the first song, Briscoe compliments Andy on his guitar playing, saying, "Doggone Sheriff, you sure can render!" Andy suggests they do another and Charlene suggests "Salty Dog" as it has some "romantic" in it. Charlene sings the song with her brothers sometimes joining in. She dances a few steps while singing. As she sings, she playfully takes the lit pipe out of her brother's mouth who is playing the upright bass then puts it back. She then pulls the banjo player's hat down onto his head. After taking a flower from a vase in the cell, she kneels down by Andy and tickles him under the chin with the flower while Briscoe watches disapprovingly out of the corner of his eye. (This scene has at least been viewed in full by many Mayberry fans as it is available on YouTube.)

The final edit is the most extreme. The epilogue is missing. In most of the edited versions, the story ends with Charlene and Dud running off happily together with Briscoe and the boys walking after them. In the missing epilogue, Andy acts as Justice of the Peace and marries Charlene and Dud. When Briscoe asks how much he owes for the service, Andy says it is usually two dollars but he will settle for a song. Briscoe suggests something nice and sentimental for a wedding like "Keep Your Money in Your Shoes and It Won't Get Wet" but they don't play it as Charlene says the song makes her cry. Andy suggests the song "Cindy" and starts it off himself. Charlene and Dud continue to hug and kiss as Andy and the Darling men play the song.

YEARS
OF
MAYBERRY

A CELEBRATION OF THE ANDY GRIFFITH SHOW

Featuring essays, recollections, and reflections

- Edited By -
RANDY TURNER

60 Years of Mayberry includes writings by Dixie Griffith, George Lindsey Jr., Bruce Bilson (Assistant Director on the series) LeRoy McNees (musical guest star), Sean Dietrich (author and *Sean of the South* creator), Allan Newsome (Floyd the Barber tribute artist and host of the *Two Chairs, No Waiting* podcast), Tim Bradshaw (author and Mayberry fan), Chris Grewe (Pastor), and Randy Turner (author and Mayberry historian). *192 pages, perfect bound*

The Mayberry Travel Guide is perfect for the Mayberry fan who is interested in the influence of Andy Griffith's hometown on his beloved TV series. It is more than just a travel guide, packed with trivia and information about both Mount Airy, North Carolina and *The Andy Griffith Show*. *384 pages, perfect bound*

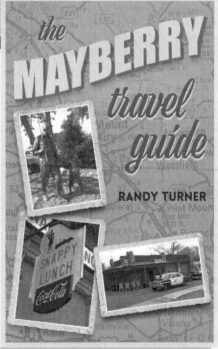

RANDY TURNER